THE
KONDRATIEFF
WAVE

THE KONDRATIEFF WAVE

JAMES B. SHUMAN
AND DAVID ROSENAU

WORLD PUBLISHING
TIMES MIRROR
NEW YORK

Published by The World Publishing Company
Published simultaneously in Canada
by Nelson, Foster & Scott Ltd.
First printing—1972
Copyright © 1972 by James B. Shuman and David Rosenau
ISBN 0-529-04561-3
Library of Congress catalog card number: 70-183091
Printed in the United States of America
Designed by Jacques Chazaud

WORLD PUBLISHING
TIMES MIRROR

CONTENTS

PREFACE

During the 1950s no one believed America's problems could not be solved, and the nation floated on a sea of self-satisfied complacency. During the 1960s that sea began to boil. Beginning with the civil rights movement, progressing through the youth revolution and the antiwar movement, wracked by the most severe inflation in fifty years, America seemed ready to explode. Challenged and confronted, some Americans resisted all change. Others tried a variety of experiments—ranging from political activism to drop-out communes—aimed at somehow forcing an improvement in the quality of life. The country became polarized. By the end of the decade, nearly everyone felt an unaccustomed sense of impotence and frustration.

Most of what happened during the 1960s, including

the Vietnam War and the social unrest that preceded and accompanied it, could have been predicted, just as a cooling off during the 1970s can be predicted. That prediction, which we first made in 1965, is based not on a projection of current trends but on a little-known economic wave, first observed shortly after World War I by the Russian economist Nikolai D. Kondratieff.

This book is an explanation of Kondratieff's theory and its implications. It shows how the long economic wave, which lasts approximately fifty-two years, has operated throughout American history and how it will operate in the future. This will doubtless be a controversial book. In an age that still relies on a narrow definition of scientific proof, a long wave that controls not only the economy but the way people act smacks too much of the occult to win the approval of rigidly scientific economists. Science, however, is now learning that some things cannot be explained "scientifically," that empirical evidence sometimes must be accepted as proof, and that cycles do exist in many facets of our lives.

The Kondratieff theory enjoyed a brief flourish of interest during the 1930s, but never caught hold. It could not compete with the immediate practicality of Keynesian theory, which offered feasible solutions, and most economists felt there had not yet been enough evidence to prove its existence.

We believe that now, as America passes the peak of another Kondratieff wave, there is enough evidence that the wave exists and that the theory should be reexamined. It is our hope that this book will encourage that reexamination. Like radar warning a ship of storms ahead, knowledge of the wave and its effects could tell us of the heavy weather our nation faces and help us plan for it so that we can minimize its effects.

JAMES B. SHUMAN *and* DAVID ROSENAU

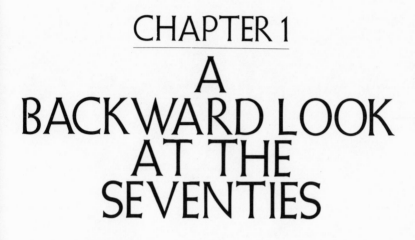

CHAPTER 1

A BACKWARD LOOK AT THE SEVENTIES

The turnout for the presidential election of 1982 was the largest in American history. After ten years of indifference the American voter suddenly awoke to the fact that this, the first major election of the new decade, would perhaps be the most important in American history. Despite reassurances by the incumbent Republican President, business was in worse shape than ever before and unemployment, which had been climbing for more than two years, now stood at 10 percent. Other indicators of economic health were down; it was clear that America's once booming economy was in a state as bad as or perhaps worse than the depression of the 1930s and that it had been heading that way for several years.

It had taken quite a while to realize the existence of

this depression. Even the newsmagazines, always so quick to analyze and amplify the pulse of America, missed the depression's early stages. Their 1979 year-end editions—devoted largely to the decade then ending—were full of optimism for the decade to come. "The 'Golden Seventies,' the century's best decade," they said, would be followed by the " 'Euphoric Eighties,' a period of even greater growth, prosperity, and happiness."

It was easy to understand their optimism. Compared with the 1960s, the 1970s had been a golden period. It was almost as if the nearly forgotten spirit of the Woodstock Nation, the last great rock music festival of the 1960s—a gathering billed as a "festival of peace, love, and music" that would usher in a new age of harmony —had in fact influenced the decade that followed.

America, like a child who outgrows the conflicts of early adolescence, did enter a period of peace early in the 1970s. It was at peace with itself, able to tolerate all the internal forces that only a few years before had threatened to rip the country apart. It was at peace, too, with the world. It is true that troubles still cropped up in Asia, Africa, and the Middle East, but the American people remained undisturbed. They retreated into semi-isolation, reluctant to get involved again in foreign entanglements, content to let the problems resolve themselves.

Many said this was a reaction to the disastrous experience of the Vietnam War. For many Americans those war years had been unhappy and disturbing times. They were characterized by such phenomena as rampant inflation, labor strife, riots, bombings, youth revolution, the near breakdown of many public services, agitation for equal rights for Blacks, concern for the poor, and a marked change in values among much of the population.

But, as the 1970s unfolded, these and other problems faded. The youth revolution became less an issue as the activists of the 1960s grew up and society began to accept many of their ideas. The generation gap that had preoccupied the public in the late 1960s narrowed as the desire to look, act, and, in fact, *be* young had, for many people, replaced acceptance of the stability and ponderous responsibilities of middle age. Moreover the new wave of young—those who were ten or twelve years behind the protesters and the rioters of the late 1960s—were the beneficiaries of the philosophy that being young was special. Having little to rebel against, they took their place in a society that had begun, at least partially, to accept their ideas.

Other problems of the 1960s dissolved in the following decade much the same way. Management of the environment, which once seemed a nearly insoluble task, proved easily done as vast amounts of money, combined with legislation, specially focused taxes, and growing social consciousness on the part of business chewed into the problems and turned the tide. The polarization of domestic politics similarly faded from view. The wide gap between conservatives and liberals narrowed as the severity of problems eased.

The easing of tensions was partly due to yet another phenomenon. The federal budget, which had been running deficits for all but six of the preceding forty-two years, began to run a modest surplus nearly every year. Except for the almost stilled voices of balanced-budget buffs, advocates of the sound dollar and of fiscal sanity, most people paid little attention. Yet balancing the budget was a key to America's new harmony, not because it meant a return to an ideological position but because of what it represented in terms of orderly management of the nation's economy.

Beginning at just about the time Richard Nixon ran for reelection in 1972, the Vietnam War had deescalated enough so that the economy, now vigorous and fully recovered from the recession of 1970–1971, could generate sufficient revenue to put the federal books modestly in the black for the fiscal year ending in June of 1973. Pessimists had said that this would not happen. They maintained that even when the United States had gotten out of the war, other needs—social welfare, urban problems, ecology, and the urgent need to improve the quality of life that had deteriorated even for the relatively affluent—would eat up funds faster than they could be collected. This was not the case. Much money was spent, of course, but even more was collected as the postwar economy boomed.

The surpluses also marked the start of a new trend in American economic policy. The economist and the man in the street had long accepted the idea that some degree of inflation was necessary for economic growth. But the more than 5-percent annual inflation of the Vietnam War years had put all wage earners under pressure from which they saw no escape. It seemed they were on a continually rising spiral in which each wage increase forced a rise in prices, which necessitated another wage increase, which forced another rise in prices.

The surpluses of the 1970s turned the tide. Federal deficits had been caused by demands for more than the economy could produce. Surpluses were a sign that everyone was demanding just a little bit less, thus allowing the superheated economic situation of the late 1960s to cool. But it did not stop there. As soon as government finances ran in the black for two years in a row, the pressure to cut taxes began. "Cutting taxes will stimulate the economy," leading economists said. They were right. Not only did business boom, the federal budget surplus for the first year under the lower tax structure was larger than when taxes were higher.

It seemed too good to be true. But it was true, and when taxes were cut again two years later, the federal budget again ran a surplus. People began to wonder why no one had thought of such tax cuts before. Their wonder did not persist, however; the surpluses continued past the end of the decade, but public interest in them did not. By the end of Richard Nixon's second term, most Americans took the surpluses for granted, just as they took for granted the end of inflation that accompanied the surpluses. For inflation, too, eased. Although most prices did not actually decline, they did stop rising, and better products or improvements in existing products came on the market at prices lower than those of the items they replaced.

The 1970s also brought a steady improvement in

public services, restoring them to the efficiency and complaint-free operation they had displayed in the 1950s. This, too, made life in America more enjoyable. For many people, especially those living in or near the great megalopolises, one of the causes of frustration in the 1960s had been the undependability of all the little things—for example, the telephones that did not work, the trains and airplanes that were late, and the mail that took two weeks to go six blocks.

Moreover, as these seemingly little things got worse, they fed a pessimism that predicted an increasingly dark future for America. At the end of the Soaring Sixties writers, economists, and commentators peered into the decade of the seventies and saw only gloom. "No way out," they said. "America is in for more trouble in the years ahead. Just look at the way society has disintegrated in the sixties. If things had gotten so bad from the solid base of the placid fifties, how could they get better from the shattered base of the sixties?" But things did get better. The prophets of gloom had not foreseen several important developments. One was the effect of money. John Kenneth Galbraith, the Harvard economist and social critic, had the foresight to see that the problems of the 1970s could be solved if both the government and the private sector of the economy would spend enough money to attack them. But even Galbraith was pessimistic; he doubted the money would ever be spent. Commenting in an interview in *New York* magazine on the plight of the nation's large cities, he said, ". . . there is the terrible tendency to think that sociology is a substitute for money. I have no doubt that nearly all, not quite all, but nearly all, of the problems of New York and Chicago, Boston, Philadelphia, and even Los Angeles—could be solved by the simple device of spending enough money: Spending it on the school system, the police, garbage collection, public housing, mass transit, on public recreation, the parks, public entertainment. But on every single one of these things there is a most stringent shortage of funds."

The money came, however. It came with the end of significant American involvement in Vietnam, with a growing distaste for any similar foreign involvement in the future, and with the disenchantment with the military machine that had grown up as a reaction to cold-war fears. This disenchantment led Congress systematically to prune the military's financial root system. This in turn released billions of dollars in revenue and thousands of talented engineers, researchers, and managers whose talents could be used to improve the quality of life.

In retrospect it was amazing what the public had been willing to put up with, and for how long. It was incredible that public support for a foreign military adventure would enable the Pentagon to tap off $30 billion a year to "save" a people most Americans had never heard of before 1965 and ten years later few ever wanted to hear of again. Few advocates of the Vietnam War ever really cared about the Vietnamese. They were more interested in "stopping the spread of communism." Those actually concerned about the Vietnamese advocated ending the war.

Every American President has tried to end wars as

rapidly as possible, for he must worry about retaining public support. Lyndon Johnson had a majority in favor of the war, but lost it. He had inherited an impossible situation, then listened to bad advice; he ignored not only the military impossibility of "winning" in Southeast Asia, but also the economic effect the war would have on the United States. In the end the attempt to have both guns and butter dug his political grave.

The reason was simple: when Johnson took office in 1963, the American economy was in an unusual position. His predecessor had run on a pledge to "get the country moving again" and the economy was poised on the edge of a major upward thrust. Guns and butter might have worked in the weak economy of 1958, but by 1965 the combination spelled disaster. Pushed beyond its ability to produce goods and services for both rapidly expanding civilian demands and rapidly expanding demands for military goods, the economic machine overheated and prices rose like the water temperature in a laboring automobile. Johnson lost control, lost support, and did not even run for reelection in 1968.

The election of Richard M. Nixon marked a watershed in American politics. Nixon formed a new coalition composed of people who, for different reasons and from different points of view, were reacting to the pressure of change, the impermanence of life in prosperous times, and the feeling of insecurity that prosperity creates in those not accustomed to it. Nixon allied southern conservatives, northern traditionalists, a prosperous laboring class, some lower-income groups pinched by inflation, and a scattering of others. But he got his crucial support from the independent middle: the people whose votes reflect their feelings rather than ideological consistency. America had swung toward conservatism, and Nixon, two-time loser, suddenly became Richard M. Nixon, President of the United States. This does not just happen; there must be reasons and, remarkably enough, the reasons are closely tied to the whole development of the period.

At first, the 1970s were an era of the conservative and of conservatism, an era of John Mitchell, Spiro Agnew, the southern strategy, and of a great national polarization between liberals and conservatives. But by the mid-seventies this split had ended. There was no return to liberalism; the disputes that marked the early 1970s simply disappeared as the issues, the problems, and the frustrations that had generated intense feelings seemed to evaporate. America did not return to the isolationism of the 1920s and 1930s, but by the end of the decade it was no longer more concerned with international affairs than with national affairs, and it seemed to have abandoned the idea of using its own military force to "rescue" nations threatened by communist take-overs. Although some of this energy was diverted to attacking the problems of cities threatened with inundation from garbage, rats, poverty, and organized crime, and to solving the problems of the environment, transportation, and the poor, most of it was diverted to improving the quality of life. The balance had tipped away from military and space hardware and foreign crusades. If people cared about things beyond their own lives, it seemed that they did not care much.

The reasons behind this shift in national mood were so obscure that it is easy to explain why the shift was not anticipated. Most commentators on American life failed to weigh correctly three things about the public attitude:

* Attitudes shift rapidly, often turning 180 degrees in response to changing conditions, particularly economic conditions.

* Attitudes may not be what surface impressions convey, no matter how clear-cut they appear, and are therefore subject to misinterpretation.

* Attitudes toward most issues are highly if not solely subjective; if someone's attitude toward something is to be assessed accurately, it is vital to see that something as he sees it, not necessarily as it is.

No group more dramatically illustrates these points than the hard hats, as construction workers who took a hard line on the Vietnam War and, later, all working-class conservatives with any "hard" in their rightward leanings were dubbed. If, in 1970, you had scratched a hard hat, you would have found a former Democrat. If he was over fifty, he had voted for Franklin D. Roosevelt; if under fifty, his father had. Roosevelt's forgotten man, as James Reston of *The New York Times* pointed out, had, in the 1968 campaign, become Nixon's forgotten people. When the rising tide of prosperity during the 1960s gave the blue-collar worker a solid standard of living, he began to feel that change (which is the promise of political liberalism) had increasingly less to offer. Finally he came to regard it as an outright threat to his recently acquired way of life. The hard hat had arrived at the place he had always wanted to be, and the prospect of further change appeared to hold nothing but the destruction of that place. This had little to do with the flag, with patriotism, or with protecting the freedom of a minority of the Vietnamese people; yet these were *supposed to be* issues that formed what was *supposed to be* the hard-hat attitude.

That the Wall Street hard-hat riots of the early 1970s were attacks on students was not because the students advocated withdrawal from Vietnam. It was because the students were viewed as liberals or radicals and therefore advocates of destructive change; it was because students were seen as intellectuals, a group that the American working class has always distrusted; it was because the working man was feeling the effects of prosperity—a fast pace, impermanence, unfamiliar affluence, and a general disappearance of the old values. Alvin Toffler† believed that these people were experiencing "future shock," and that this was a product of the time. In reality, they were experiencing the tensions brought about by prosperity, tensions created when an entire society begins to live better because everyone can spend more.

Such complex factors were overlooked by writers, economists, urbanologists, and others who gazed into the future and came away discouraged. Two decades of prosperity had not only changed everything; they had

---

†Alvin Toffler, "New York Faces Future Shock," *New York* magazine, July 27, 1970, p. 20.

also put the country in poor economic shape to fight the Vietnam War. There was no surplus capacity to devote to war. The war provided economic stimulation *on top of prosperity;* it was too much of a good thing. In such a frenzied climate, clear perspective was difficult.

By the end of Nixon's second term, however, America was a far different place than it had been in 1970. Not only had the tangible problems begun to disappear, but also some of the intangible ones had as well. One of the first to go after the Vietnam War ended was the generation gap. While the Vietnam War was still being fought and before air pollution, water pollution, racial and sex discrimination had received the attention and the money needed to deal with them effectively, young people had assumed a committed posture—committed to change and improvements. But what do old (or no longer young) war protesters do when the war is over? Is it possible to stay committed, to be antiestablishment when that establishment begins to right injustices and takes meaningful steps to save the environment? One cannot simply continue hurling epithets at people who not only admit they have been wrong, but take steps to correct their mistakes. So the stance of the youths of the 1960s, the Woodstock Generation, softened. They *had* helped to remake the world, or at least a part of it.

In the post-Vietnam years, the young people were generally at peace with their elders. By 1976 the seventeen-, twenty-, and twenty-two-year-olds were too concerned with the quest for a better life, with the enjoyment of the good things in a society in which things worked and got done, to be the rebels their thirty-year-old brothers had been. Not that the young had no complaints in the last half of the 1970s. They did. But their causes were neither as consuming nor as polarized as those that inflamed the latter part of the 1960s.

One cause that still divided the country was whether marijuana should be legalized. It had started as a cause among the young in the 1960s, and the cause spread as they grew older and as they introduced it to other adults who were their seniors. Actually its use was so common by the latter half of the seventies that *cause* was not the right word. Rather, it was as fashionable as drinking, and like those before them who drank during Prohibition, a large number of the people had simply become scofflaws. As the use of marijuana spread, the absurdity of this "new Prohibition" became embarrassingly obvious. Legislatures that had written the original laws regarding drugs had failed to differentiate between hard drugs and marijuana and between pushers and users. Moreover they had thrown in a heavy dose of righteous indignation toward "dope fiends" and had spewed forth harsh penalties: for possession alone, one could get up to life imprisonment in Texas. These laws had been on the books long before marijuana usage had become common, and in the 1970s it was obvious that they could not survive. Nebraska was the first state to lower the penalties for possession of marijuana. New Jersey followed suit. By the end of the decade most states had voted similar changes, making the punishment for possession no more severe than that for disturbing the peace.

In the 1970s the ideals, customs, tastes, clothes, music, manners, and whenever possible the attitudes of the young began to be copied by older groups in society. This trend began at the end of the 1960s; it first appeared at universities and other places where adults were in contact with the young, then spread outward until what had started as a trickle ended as a torrent. Nothing more clearly shows the overall shift in outlook than the gradual acceptance of marijuana.

This shift in outlook was similar to the kind of change that has always swept in on the tide of prosperity throughout American history. The years just prior to the escalation of the war in Vietnam, like the years just before World War I, marked the beginning of changes that were felt with broadening impact all through the seventies and represented a second major swing away from Victorianism. The first swing had begun almost as soon as Queen Victoria died in 1901; it gathered momentum through the next two decades and became a widespread, established phenomenon during the 1920s. With the Great Depression of the 1930s, however, the bastions of a more rigid code were manned once again, not to come under serious attack again until the 1960s when society, perhaps led by the young, began to swing. Much of it was of course vicarious, but the shift had taken place: things that once were "not discussed" were openly flaunted, and movies, books, advertising, and television began to mirror what people felt they would like to do, even if they did not actually do it.

Other tensions also began to dissolve in the prosperous, postwar 1970s. Living the good life, becoming a fulfilled individual became the prime goal of most people, in contrast to the political preoccupations of the 1960s. But merely trying to be happy was not enough. One had to appear happy as well, and in that liberated age anyone who was not liberated was, by definition, not happy. Being liberated was something one could work at; being happy was only a result. It meant that, to those willing to actively pursue their liberation, certain conventional things—not swearing, wearing a tie to work, and fitting into a mold—became anachronisms. To flaunt convention insured one that he would be easily recognizable as "with it," aware of the enjoyments life held for the taking, and unlike the "establishment straights." Such attitudes were infectious.

Women, particularly, began to show changes in their patterns of speech and attitudes. Rather than building on their initial success to force significant reforms in legislation, education, and public opinion to ensure truly equal status, however, many women, revelling in new-found freedoms, such as the right to enter once all-male restaurants, settled for the illusion that equality had been gained. As women felt freer to do and say what they wanted, the results were often extreme—and often a little sad.

By the end of the 1970s, it was clear that the attitudes of the nation had been transformed. The bitter controversies that characterized the earlier years had slipped away, and with them went the whole preoccupation with politics, revolution, law and order, and foreign involvement. Although some of the nation's problems were solved, many were not; but they were simply ig-nored. One could not be apocalyptic in one's outlook for the future because the decade had been too good to everyone. No one would buy a pessimistic forecast about the 1980s, so none was made. America, it seemed, was in control of itself, its resources, and its problems.

Although there was nothing identifiably wrong, America was heading toward trouble. The nation was finishing the decade on a good note, having recovered from a mild business slowdown in 1978. There had been only one other downturn, also very mild, since the recession of 1970–1971. Before both recessions, the Federal Reserve System had tightened money, and in both cases the result was a mild contraction followed by tax cuts that stimulated the economy. These midcourse corrections worked perfectly on the newly docile economy. After the 1960s, when the economy had seemed uncontrollable, it was at first a pleasant surprise and later an expectation that something as complex as the American economy could be so carefully managed.

America entered the 1980s with an optimism not seen for a long time. How, people asked, could the eighties be anything but an exceptionally good decade, an extension of the era that had begun in the early seventies? The eighties started out well. Interest rates and commodity prices turned up slightly. The federal budget, which had run a surplus in every year since 1973, continued to run in the black. People could not have cared less about the state of the economy. Things were so good that no one saw how they could ever go bad.

It happened slowly at first. It was late in 1980, and

there was little to indicate that anything important was happening. The leading indicators, those unexciting statistical scorecards that economists watch, began to turn down one by one. So did the stock market. Nothing to be alarmed about, the experts said. "Just some selling—a technical correction." And they promised that when it was over there would be important buying opportunities. But the selling continued. There were minor rallies but the market continued to go down.

The nation took things in stride, good-naturedly. "Perhaps the market was a bit overbought," the experts explained. "The correction would do it good—no sense in getting emotional, the market had sold off many times before and things had always turned out right." Corporate earnings figures were disappointing, but only because temporary problems had cut into profits. Money rates, though well down from their peak levels of early 1970, had turned up slightly over the past year and a half, raising costs unexpectedly. In addition, the Japanese were everywhere, providing tough competition. But there were lots of opportunities in the future. The situation was nothing to get edgy about.

But when the market decline reached 20 percent the public became edgy. Still the experts preached confidence: "It is absurd to worry; things are in too good shape," the experts said. "Remember the 1969–1970 sell-off. It had seemed staggering at the time, but it is easy to see how foolish those who panicked were, for the recession that followed was only a reaction to tight money. Although it hit certain segments very hard, it was short-lived."

But the selling continued. Again, there were minor rallies, but the trend was down. The public worried and the professionals watched for the signs of what would happen. The selling, of course, would have to stop eventually because every bear market eventually runs out of sellers. But what would happen then? There were two courses the market could take. It could slowly grind to a halt, move sideways on very low volume and then rally, or it could come to a crashing climax with huge volume and panic selling followed by a sharp rally, bouncing upward, like a tennis ball that has been smashed against the sidewalk. It bounced. After the selling climax had shaken out those who would shake, the rest, those of strong nerve, those locked in, and those too numb with fear and shock to decide, looked on while the wild, frenzied end of the selling came and the market shot back up. Ten years before, on the old exchange, the floor brokers would have begun to sing, "Wait till the sun shines Nellie," but in late 1980 the computers that now formed "the floor" of the exchange only hummed unemotionally in their windowless, air-conditioned quarters.

The stock market recovered about 65 percent of what it had lost before it began sliding again. The rally, however, had reinforced the idea that the economy was basically sound. Because the crash was considered nothing more than a sharp readjustment, the renewed downtrend was at first a disappointment, then as the selling again became relentless it turned to despair and then to fear. The overall economy, however, did not react rapidly to the events in the market. Some early

warnings of something wrong had been given by leading indicators, but these did not foretell the magnitude
of what was to come. The economy just started to slide
and kept sliding. Inventories were cut and orders can-
celled. Workers first lost overtime, then their jobs.
Unemployment rose and the Index of Industrial Production fell. The handwriting, the experts now said, was
on the wall: the nation was in for a recession, perhaps
a fairly stiff one.

They were wrong. The nation was in for a depression.
Depression: the awful word that economists had refused
to apply to any economic downturn since the 1930s. It
would be more than two years before it was obvious,
before the situation would be serious enough for the
term to be spontaneously revived: more than 15-percent
unemployment for two successive years and a 25-per-
cent decline in industrial production and national income.

Like the Great Depression of the 1930s, no one
believed it could happen and no one could conceive
how bad it would get. What the public never understood is that there is a sharp difference between the
ability to climb out of a depression and the ability to
prevent one. We can climb out of but not prevent a
depression. Moreover, since everyone insisted it
could not happen, the economy was well on the way
to the bottom before effective countermeasures were
enacted. The "automatic stabilizers" on which the
United States had relied in the past were simply not
adequate to the task.

The downturn that followed the 1981 crash was far

more serious than the mild recessions which had occurred in the long period of prosperity that had preceded it. It was bigger and more stubborn. It smashed businesses, careers, and confidence, and it was not about to be nudged by the relatively modest federal budget deficits and easy money measures that were applied. In the 1930s, the depression had hit bottom by the time Franklin Roosevelt took office, and it was several years after the recovery began that John Maynard Keynes was able to introduce the notion of deficit spending to stimulate recovery. Even then, the kind of money the Keynesians wanted to spend was considered exorbitant. The money required to reverse the trend in the 1980s was staggering by comparison because the gross national product was twelve times as large and the President, in a time when few realized or wanted to admit the seriousness of the situation, could not suggest a deficit-spending budget large enough to be effective. It was only when things had nearly hit bottom in January 1983 that the Chief Executive went before the Congress and proposed that the government run a deficit equal to 15 percent of what the gross national product had been in 1980. No one could believe the figure: $240 billion.

It was over three years after the crash that the truly massive expenditures were voted, undertaken, and their effects began to be felt. By this time, however, the depression had run its course and the purging process that the laissez-faire philosophers had always held in such high regard had been completed. The man in the street, the man who had lost his job, or the man who lived in constant fear that he might lose his job cared little about the therapeutic effects of a purge of the economy. To him, the economy had been scrubbed against the wall and him with it.

CHAPTER 2
INTRODUCING THE LONG WAVE

A calm America, her inner conflicts quieted, again tormented by a grinding depression? How do we make such a prediction in the early 1970s? The answer is simple: There is a pattern in American history and economics that has escaped public notice, a long wave of economic expansion and contraction that has recurred throughout American history.

Most people know of business cycles; they are established phenomena. As Paul A. Samuelson of the Massachusetts Institute of Technology explains in his textbook *Economics,* a cycle is characterized when "national income, employment, and production fall. Prices and profits decline and men are thrown out of work. Eventually the bottom is reached and revival begins. The recovery may be slow or fast. It may be incomplete or it may be so strong as to lead to a new boom. The new prosperity may represent a long, sustained plateau of brisk demand, plentiful jobs, buoyant prices, and increased living standards. Or it may represent a quick, inflationary flaring up of prices and speculation, to be followed by another disastrous slump." †

The late Wesley C. Mitchell, long-time director of the nonprofit National Bureau of Economic Research, assiduous student of business cycles, and father of cycle theories, divided the waves in business activity into two major phases: the periods of expansion and contraction. Expansion comes to an end at the upper turning point, or peak. Contraction, which begins at the end of the expansion phase, lasts until the lower turning point, the trough or revival.

Economists have isolated all sorts of business cycles. One lasts approximately 8 years, another 3.51 years, another approximately 18 years. Most intriguing, however, is a cycle not all economists yet accept, for it lasts about half a century, and, as Samuelson says, "Whether these long waves are simply historical accidents due to chance gold discoveries, inventions and political wars, it is still too soon to say." Economists, however, overlook the fact there is now enough evidence and that this long wave is the most important of all, for it reflects not only major economic trends of the economy but all facets of national life—from prosperity to social unrest to involvement in foreign affairs. Moreover it is the

†Paul A. Samuelson, *Economics: An Introductory Analysis,* 5th ed. (New York: McGraw-Hill, 1961), p. 285.

strongest of all waves; other cycles act only as brakes or accelerators, strengthening or weakening but never diverting the economy.

First to spot this long wave was a Russian, Nikolai D. Kondratieff, a professor at the Agricultural Academy and head of the Business Research Institute of Moscow after the Russian Revolution. Kondratieff, analyzing prices in Germany, France, and the United States, trade in England and France, and production of coal, iron, and other products throughout the world, set forth his theory in a series of books and papers published between 1922 and 1928. He said that the Western world had experienced two and a half long waves, or upward and downward price fluctuations, since the end of the eighteenth century: the first lasted from fifty to sixty years, the second from forty to fifty years.† The third was in progress when Kondratieff wrote. By years, Kondratieff's first wave ran approximately from the end of the 1780s to 1844–1851, with a peak between 1810 and 1817. The second ran from 1844–1851 to 1890–1896, with a peak in 1870–1875. The third began in 1890–1896 , peaking in 1914–1920, when, he said, the decline "probably begins."

Critics within Russia jumped all over Kondratieff. Part of their scorn was due to the reluctance of orthodox Marxists to accept a theory that said that downturns in the capitalist economies were not due to

---

†This fluctuation does not discredit the existence of the wave. Although it may operate over a fifty-four-year period one time and a forty-nine-period the next, it is still a valid recurrence. Moreover, since some measures of economic phenomena top or bottom out before others, trying to fix an *exact* turning point in any cycle is futile.

inherent defects within the system but were self-correcting.

The Marxian view was succinctly summed up by the official *Soviet Russian Encyclopedia*. It dismissed Kondratieff's work in one sentence: "This theory is wrong and reactionary." Kondratieff himself was banished. In 1930 the Russian secret police arrested him as the alleged head of an illegal, antigovernmental Peasant's Labor Party and, without trial, shipped him to Siberia.

Others, however, have built on Kondratieff's work. The most notable was a flamboyant Austrian-born Harvard economist, Joseph Schumpeter, who compiled an exhaustive two-volume study entitled *Business Cycles,* which was published in 1939. Schumpeter developed a complete economic system of regular, cyclical growth and contraction, using what he considered the three major cycles: Kondratieff's long cycle and two others. The others, named after the men who discovered them, were the forty-month Kitchin cycle and the ten-year Juglar cycle.

In Schumpeter's scheme, the Kitchin cycle produces little serious damage or permanent change in the economy beyond its psychological effect on economists, who give so much attention to methods for compensating for short cycles (most of which seem to cure themselves quickly anyway) that they virtually ignore the cause of the longer fluctuations. The ten-year Juglar cycle is more important. It provides the link between the long Kondratieff and the short Kitchin, the logical point in the progress between the short cycle everyone knows exists and the long one that few people even suspect. Even more important, and because the Juglar turning point periodically coincides with the Kondratieff turning point, it can be used to date major turning points in the economy.

The implications are startling. As Schumpeter wrote: "No claims are made for our three cycle scheme except that it is a useful descriptive or illustrative device. Using it, however, in that capacity, we in fact got *ex visu* of 1929, a 'forecast' of a serious depression embodied in the formula: coincidence of depression phases of all three cycles."†

To understand best how the Kondratieff wave works, however, we must set up a simple model. As a basis for this model we will use the federal government's Wholesale Commodity Price Index, a measure of fluctuations in the prices of such items as standard farm products, processed foods and feeds, industrial commodities, and consumer finished goods. Generally considered a more accurate reflection of business conditions than the more commonly known Consumer Price Index, it does not include such things as the cost of services (labor) or finished products, which lag behind the cost of raw materials. Later we will flesh out the model with other events and trends which occur at specific places in each wave.

Let us look first at a typical swing of the Wholesale Commodity Price Index. Starting at a peak, there is a sharp drop, then for about a decade a sideways wiggling

†Joseph A. Schumpeter, *Business Cycles* (New York: McGraw Hill, 1939), vol. I, p. 174.

or slight drop; then there is a sharp fall again at the end of that first decade, with a continuing decline for two more decades. The bottom is reached three decades after the peak, then prices run for two decades to another peak, approximately fifty-two years after the preceding peak.

The test of a model, of course, is whether it works in actual practice. So let us look at wholesale commodity prices, starting during the War of 1812, the first period when business statistics were reliable enough to be useful. The War of 1812 came at the peak in prices, the Wholesale Commodity Price Index (in 1958 dollars) reaching 62.3 in 1814. In 1819 there was a sharp recession, with the index falling to 47.7. Then there was a very gradual decline, interrupted occasionally by slight increases, until the index reached a bottom of 25.4 in 1843. At this point prices turned upward and continued upward until the end of the Civil War. The Civil War, of course, took place about five decades after the War of 1812. The action of prices during those five decades was a downtrend for three decades and an uptrend for the next two.

The Civil War, like the War of 1812, represented a period of peak prices: prices climbed for two decades before the war, reaching a high on the Wholesale Commodity Price Index of 74.7 in 1864. The most intense inflation came during the war, with prices more than doubling. After the Civil War, prices behaved exactly as they had after the War of 1812, maintaining a thirty-year downward trend from 1865 to 1896, when they reached a low of 25.4. Then they moved up again for about two decades, through the World War I period.

Now let us try the price portion of our model. If you were to make an overlay out of this model, a wartime peak followed by three decades of decline and about two decades of a rising trend with another peak during another war, you could use it to describe either the period from the War of 1812 to the Civil War *or* the period from the Civil War to World War I.

How does the model hold up from World War I to the present? On the whole, very well. If we overlay our model on actual prices from the World War I peak to the present, we find that it conforms well from the peak (which actually occurred in 1920, just after the war) through the late 1930s. However, after nearly two decades of a declining price trend, a combination of New Deal programs and the huge armament expenditures that began just prior to World War II (probably chiefly the latter) reversed the trend about a decade early. The model indicates that the trend should have reversed about 1950. Actually, it did so about ten years earlier. From 1950 on, however, the model resumes its accuracy. There are two decades of gradually rising prices, with another sharp peak (the fourth in a row) predicted for about 1970, following a period of sharply rising prices.

Before going into more precise detail about the actions of prices, let us examine some of the events or trends that are part of the model, that is, things that happen at the same relative time in each five-decade span covered by the model. One of the most startling is that a war has appeared with each price peak and that these wars had an enormous influence on prices. The dates of these peak wars and the periods between were:†

	War began	Period between peak wars
WAR OF 1812	1812	1812 TO 1861 (49 years)
CIVIL WAR	1861	1861 TO 1914 (53 years)
WORLD WAR I	1914	1914 TO 1965 (49 years)
VIETNAM WAR	1965	

There have, of course, been other American wars besides the ones that occurred at price peaks, but they too—with one exception, World War II—fell at predictable points in the wave. The first war following the War of 1812 was the Mexican War, which started in 1846, at a trough in the wave, just *after* the price trend had reversed its thirty-year decline from the peak in 1814. If the model is going to work for wars, we would expect a war just after *each* trough in prices, and since we have a model with a time span of just over fifty years, there should be "trough" war approximately every five decades. If we overlay the model on the next period (from the Civil War peak to the World War I peak) there should have been a war at about the same relative

†You may argue that American involvement in World War I did not begin until 1917 and that, technically, there were some American troups in Vietnam prior to 1965, but it would be quibbling to say that the dates listed are not reasonably representative of the beginnings of *serious* hostilities.

place some fifty years after the Mexican War, or just after the 1896 price bottom. And of course, there was. The Spanish-American War broke out in 1897, fifty-one years after the Mexican War. Checking forward to the third segment (World War I to Vietnam), we would expect to find a war about five decades after the Spanish-American War. We do. The Korean War broke out in 1950, fifty-three years later.

The deviation of World War II, the only exception from the periodicity of other wars, does not affect the basic premise. We are *not* implying that there has never been, or could never be, a war that does not fit our model. What we *are* saying is that there has been a war at each peak and trough, and that both the peak and the trough wars occur about every fifty years.

There are, as we implied earlier, a number of things that happen at specific points in the model. Wholesale commodity price movements and the rise and fall of interest rates may sound boring, abstract, and impersonal, but these prices are representative of all prices and easily translate into more personally relevant things such as the intense inflation that gripped the United States during 1969 and 1970 and severely strained millions of personal budgets. Interest rates, too, are the price of a special commodity—money—and when you negotiate a mortgage at 8½ percent at one point in the model and at 5 percent at another, you are feeling the effect firsthand. Economics may sound distant and esoteric, but if you were one of the many unemployed during the recession of 1970–1971 you would have found it of more than passing interest that this recession was predictable fifty years before it happened.

Let us introduce a few of these things into our model. First, take interest rates, the price of money. One would expect that interest rates would rise when other prices rose and would fall as those prices fell. Looking back from the time of the Civil War to the present, we find this assumption to be true. Interest rates fell and rose with commodity prices. There was a slight lag at times —never more than two years—when interest rates trailed prices, but in general the wholesale commodity price movements that form the basis of our model also describe the movements of interest rates since the Civil War. Rate information for the years before the Civil War, particularly for the early years of the nineteenth century, is too incomplete to be reliable, but there is nothing in the limited information available to indicate that the movement of interest rates during that period was not sympathetic with price movements.

Just as the wars that occurred after two decades of rising prices represented price peaks, so were they periods of interest-rate peaks. The Civil War, the first peak for which there are good records, was a difficult war to finance and it was financed at high rates of interest. Just as the federal government's bidding for goods and services forced prices up in an intense inflationary spiral, so, too, did governmental bidding for money to buy those goods and services force interest rates up just as rapidly, setting records that would stand for years. Lincoln's secretary of the treasury, Salmon P. Chase, not only failed to estimate the needs of financing the war, but he was also working against an uphill trend of rates. This has always been the case with peak wars; because of other demands on the economy, they are difficult to finance and money is unusually expensive. After the war, however, interest rates fell and over the next three decades the lows were successively lower, while the highs continually failed to reach their previous levels.

There is, of course, no one rate of interest. But a composite of high-quality railroad bonds, the blue chips of their day, were representative of the post–Civil War period, for there were few sizable industrial corporations around. These bonds fell from over 6 percent to just under 3 percent in the thirty years after the Civil War. Then, just as wholesale commodity prices had bottomed in 1896, interest rates hit their low in 1898.

The Spanish-American War began in 1897, just after prices bottomed out, and it was an easy war to finance. It was short and inexpensive. It also took place after the economy had been deflating for three decades, when money was plentiful and therefore cheap. Although the war had almost no noticeable effect on interest rates, they were to climb for two decades after the war. They reached a peak in 1920 and exhibited, during World War I, the same effects they had exhibited during the Civil War—thus fitting the basic model of approximately three decades of decrease and about two of increase.

The model describes interest rates pretty well from World War I to the present. In fact it works better for money rates than for commodity prices because the government firmly controlled interest rates during

World War II, and the decade of distortion that that war created in the commodity price model is not present in money rates. Interest rates actually bottomed out in 1946 and remained virtually unchanged until 1950. From 1950 on, of course, they rose to the very sharp peak associated with the Vietnam War, which is exactly what the model predicted they would do. The Korean conflict, which occurred in the same relative position in the model as the Mexican and Spanish-American wars, was, like those earlier wars, relatively easy to finance (the Truman administration ran a surplus in 1951) and had little effect on interest rates. This is also what the model indicates should have happened.

Now that we have examined the period since the Civil War by laying two models end to end (this covers just slightly more than one century), we will turn back to the period prior to the Civil War interest-rate peak. As we said earlier, information on interest rates before the Mexican War (1846) is too sketchy to use, but we do have a reasonable picture of the financing of the war and the action of rates from there on. Briefly stated, the war was easy to finance and interest rates were low, just as was the case with the Spanish-American and Korean wars. (This of course fits the model.) After the war, rates rose to their Civil War peaks.

What does all this mean? Suppose that in 1950 you knew that interest rates would soon begin to rise and would keep rising until the early 1970s. If you had wanted to manage your money wisely, you would have become a borrower rather than a lender. That would have meant you would have kept your money out of savings accounts, government and corporate bonds, and most forms of insurance. People who bought common stocks two decades ago did better than those who bought fixed interest bonds. But those who borrowed and bought income-producing property did best of all because they borrowed and bought when the prices were low and in later years, as prices and interest rates rose, income from these investments and capital values rose, but the amount of money borrowed and their interest rates stayed fixed. Today this all seems very obvious, but at the time popular belief was that as soon as the pent-up wartime demand had been satisfied, the economy was going to turn down again; that deflation, not inflation, was the threat.

Today few people believe that inflationary pressures will ever ease. Even conservative economists talk only of reducing the rate of inflation, not stopping inflation itself. Yet the Kondratieff theory indicates that inflation will stop, for over the past 156 years prices and interest rates have fallen and risen in an exact pattern three times. Moreover each time they rose to a peak it was during a period of economic turmoil and social upheaval associated with a war, first the War of 1812, then the Civil War, then World War I, and finally the Vietnam War. Each of these wars was difficult to finance and persisted longer than anticipated by those who optimistically pushed the country to war under slogans promising "to save the American way of life," "to make all men free," "to make the world safe for democracy," or "to stop the spread of communism." Each war became politically unpopular before it ended, and the often near-chaotic economic conditions visited upon the public as the government struggled to tax, spend, and shoot away billions of dollars clearly contributed to this unpopularity. As we will see in some detail later, the riots, the bombings, and the radical politics associated with these wars and the immediate postwar years are symptomatic. Equally symptomatic is the postwar rejection of the military and the public thirst for peace and normality.

The importance of wars in the Kondratieff theory should not be overemphasized. This book will not try to predict the next war nor will it say that wars take place only after prices and interest rates fall for three decades or after they rise for two. As World War II proved, a war can occur at any time, for that war's position in the model does not fit anything that occurred in the past. But just as surely, the peak and trough wars do fit a pattern, and the probability of another war occurring at the time of the next trough—sometime in the closing years of this century—is high.

Wars, however, are just one of a number of phenomena that occur. While peak wars have an enormous impact on the economy as they are being fought, their effects disappear quickly after hostilities cease. Trough wars cause little disturbance. Without these wars, the long-term picture would probably change little. The relentless pounding the economy has taken in the series of depressions that occurred during the thirty-year trends of falling prices, the great movements and lasting changes of those years, far surpass anything born of a war. The organization of the American Federation of Labor in the early 1880s, for example, was an effort on the part of workingmen to resist further wage cuts during the period of falling prices following the Civil War. The Sherman Anti-Trust Act was enacted in 1890 after businessmen had sought to combine forces and restrict competition to halt the continuing slide of prices. Such far-reaching developments as these are clearly tied to the long wave in prices. They far exceed wars as factors involved in permanent change. It was not a war that created an income tax so high as to be nearly confiscatory in the upper brackets, nor was a war associated with the new social conscience born in the 1930s. Yet these things have profoundly influenced our lives today. Lyndon Johnson's "guns and butter" nonsense played havoc with the American economy, but Andrew Jackson's peacetime move to stop land speculation (the "specie circular" of 1836) nearly destroyed it.

It may seem that the long wave in prices has gone undetected. Actually, this is not the case. Proponents of the theory, however, have been ignored. But the facts pointing to the existence of the long wave are too consistent, the results too vivid to ignore. Professional economists have rejected the long-wave theory out of hand, probably because they have felt it is not scientific. Yet the accumulated evidence of more than 150 years, as the following chapters will prove, is too consistent to ignore.

CHAPTER 3
THE DOWNWARD SPIRAL

In the beginning, after years of rapid inflation, the deflation that marks the downward phase of the Kondratieff wave is highly attractive. Suddenly prices stop climbing; they may even fall a bit. The turmoil of the war years ends. The nation settles into peaceful equilibrium. Unfortunately it does not last. After about a decade, the economy falters. Business slackens. Unemployment rises. Wages are cut. Soon the nation finds itself in the middle of a full-scale depression. The effects are not only economic. During the downswing people are more cautious, less inclined to take risks, not just in matters involving money, but in their personal lives. When times are good there is more revelry, more willingness to experiment, to "let it all hang out." When the economy turns sour, people walk the line.

This chapter concerns the downswing of the long wave, the three decades when the trend of prices is down and the trend of depressed years is up: in short, the years of deflation to come, the years from the 1970s until the turn of the century.

During the downtrend phase prices, wages, and interest rates may rise after each recession, but they never return to their previous levels. During the downtrend there also are more business slumps and in general these are not only more severe, but they also last longer than the mild recessions of the upswing years. The downtrend years do not look the way one might envision them. Few people would recognize the first decade after the peak. For the majority of people—those not thrown out of work—the primary postwar recession is a good period, a relief from the intense inflation of the peak. In the more primitive economy of the past, this was a logical reaction to the sudden withdrawal of huge wartime demand. Such setbacks occurred in 1819 following the War of 1812, in 1865 following the Civil War, and in 1920 following World War I.

Now, as we wind down the Vietnam War and fight against the extreme inflation that it did much to create, the economy is experiencing the fourth peak-war recession. The reaction after World War I was actually aggravated by the Federal Reserve System, a remarkable feat for an institution whose role has become identified with counterbalancing the extremes in the business cycle. The recession of 1970–1971 is showing the same signs of tinkering, but this time it is far more sophisticated. The Federal Reserve, tightly restricting the nation's money supply, created a squeeze designed to slow business and halt wartime inflation. The simple act of making it nearly impossible for blue-chip industrial corporations to borrow money at a reasonable rate of interest and completely impossible for lesser creditors to borrow at any rate at all slowed business, which slowed the advance of prices. Selective cuts in military and space programs intensified the slowdown. Had the Vietnam War ended suddenly and had the Federal Reserve System continued to apply pressure, we would have had the same dangerous situation as in 1920 –1921. As it was, the recession was the longest since World War II and, for the first time in years, the casualties were significant. The Penn Central Railroad bankruptcy, which was precipitated by the combination of slowing business and tight money, is one example. It has the distinction of being the greatest failure in the history of business enterprise, although General Motors nearly went bankrupt in the 1920–1921 shake-out and was saved by the Du Pont Company, which bought 25 percent of its stock.

After the initial postwar recession comes a period with something for everyone. It is the first decade of the downswing, but it is mostly a matter of prices not going up any more, a plateau between the peak of rapidly rising prices and the canyon of their rapid fall. A period of neither inflation or deflation, it represents a kind of no-flation that comes as a relief from the wartime peak and is only a memory a decade later. We are about to experience such a time. There have been three other periods like this in our history, each after a peak war.

The first was the Era of Good Feelings, which encompassed the years immediately following the War of 1812; the next was the Reconstruction following the Civil War; the most recent was the 1920s. All of these periods had a number of things in common:

* Each lasted approximately one decade and followed a major war that had been difficult and expensive to finance, politically unpopular, and had caused a period of intense inflationary pressure.

* Each occurred about fifty years after the preceding one.

* Each was bounded on one side by a short primary postwar recession, and on the other by a much longer and relatively severe secondary postwar depression. The most severe depression in American history began in 1929, about ten years after World War I, but it was only the second longest. The longest occurred fifty-five years earlier, ten years after the Civil War, at the end of the Reconstruction. This was probably the second most severe depression in our history. The third longest depression was milder than the one in the 1870s. It marked the end of the Era of Good Feelings, lasted four years, and began in 1825—forty-nine years before the depression of 1874–1879 and about a decade after 1814, the year that the War of 1812 ended.

* Each decade following the peak wars has been the one in which the federal budget was balanced more often than any other decade of the fifty-year-long wave; political ideology seems to have had little to do with whether the federal government went in debt or not. In the three decades immediately following the past peak wars, thirty years taken together, the federal budget ran a surplus twenty-seven times and a deficit only three times. But this deficit-to-surplus ratio gradually deteriorated so that in the next two decades, the thirtieth through the fiftieth years of the wave, the budget was unbalanced most of the time. This indicates that, on the whole, it has been easier to run a federal surplus just after the wartime inflation has been terminated and revenues are high. In general the public attitude at the end of the great wars has been one of resolve to eliminate the newly swollen national debt. But after a surplus or two, after the end of hostilities, this resolve fades and taxes are cut. The tax cuts, however, have had the magic effect of increasing revenues at a time when expenditures and, to a lesser degree, prices, are falling. It stimulates the economy and deflates it at the same time. It works because the economy has been overtaxed to buy goods which were destroyed in war. During the first decade, pent-up civilian wants are satisfied by turning the output of the economy back to civilian needs. The tax money that formerly went to the government is returned to the consumer to spend. Times are good because inflationary pressures are no longer stealing buying power, because money is plentiful, and because industry is working at full capacity to fill the demands postponed during the wartime inflation.

* Each post-peak-war period has provided relief from the intense pressures of the war years, which always come on the heels of two decades of gradually rising prices, rising economic prosperity, and rising excitement. The nation's whole psychology changes. The

relatively high level of prosperity, the stable or gradually falling price level, combined with the increased
buying power generated by lower taxes, contributes to
a feeling of well-being. But it is more than this. It is a
time when America psychologically has returned home
and back to business—back to the basic preoccupations
and satisfactions of personal lives and careers, a turning
away from the issues of the great wars, the great crusades. The emotions of the war years always disappear
as rapidly as the financial woes. The riots associated
with the Civil War and those that took place just after
the end of World War I were in sharp contrast to the
events of the decades that followed, as the public lost
its passion for politics and its stomach for war. The riots
of the Vietnam War years will undoubtedly be followed
by such a reaction. The demonstrations, the bombings,
the confrontations of today will disappear not so much
because the issues will have been resolved, but because
the tensions will have eased. The years of the peak wars
and the wars themselves have always been charged with
emotion.

In the years before the peak, tensions build with the
excitement of prosperity. The great issues that develop
are both national and multinational. In 1812 it was
America, supported by the French, against Great Brit-
ain; later, the North against the South; and then, America and the Allies against Germany. In Vietnam it has
been the American army against the intangible menace
of international communism. There have also been
other issues woven in. Civil rights for blacks, for example, cropped up first in the 1850s and again 100 years

later. It was no accident that the issue appeared at exactly the same relative point in the wave the second time. The issue and the deep-seated passions it engendered sprung up in the prewar climate of the 1960s, just as they did prior to the Civil War. Women's liberation last appeared fifty years before the recent movement, under the same conditions, around the end of World War I. The long-wave peak, then, is also an emotional peak, a time when pent-up repressions gush out in a kind of national catharsis. When it is over, the country seemingly has gotten it out of its system and returns to a state of equilibrium, having changed but not radically.

The decade that follows this emotional upheaval and its subsequent turning point probably represents the way people would like life to be. It cannot last, however, for there is no such thing as sustaining a perfectly balanced situation. The economy cannot remain stable like a billiard ball motionless on a level table; it must move. In the 1970s that table will shift its balance from a position where it is tipped toward inflation, through the balance point, and then be tipped, very slightly, toward deflation. This shift process will be subtle and will go wholly unnoticed. It will not, however, go unfelt.

We have said that the first decades following the wartime peaks have been good years, times when people believed they were getting back to what life should be all about. For the man in the street the emotional impact has run the gamut from prewar tension, to wartime frustration, to a brief postwar recession brush with insecurity, to an economic plateau where wages and purchasing power begin to catch up with pent-up needs and desires. Memories are short and after half a decade of what seems to be prosperity stabilized at a high level, the incidents of the hectic peak years will seem almost unreal, just as the possibility of their occurrence might have seemed before the peak. It is our incredible shortness of memory that helps us believe that the present will always be extrapolated into the future. It also helps people believe that the trend of current events is somehow not only logical but can be foreseen, that if the economy is prosperous now, it always will be. But these trends seldom continue.

The secondary postwar depressions, the ones that have always followed the prosperous postwar decade, have always been the most unexpected; they also have been the most stubborn and the most severe. In these periods things did not move gradually from good times to bad; they moved rapidly, from ideal times to disaster. Few people have the resilience (or the resources) to cope with such extreme and rapid swings.

While there is no clear explanation of why the price downswing gets started in the first place, exhibits a periodicity, or lasts as long as it does, it is possible to analyze with some clarity what happens while the downtrend is in effect. Take the situation of a manufacturer, as an example. Let us say he sets up a business at the exact peak of the long wave. He uses the traditional capital structure of some equity financing and some debt to build a plant capable of producing a fixed amount of goods. He borrows $10 million at 9 percent by issuing twenty-five-year bonds. A decade or so later a competitor builds a more modern plant for the same price or maybe less. In addition the competitor borrows his money at 7 percent. The net result is that the new arrival in business not only has a better plant, but he has lower overhead, making it possible to sell the manufactured product at a lower cost. The first manufacturer must then cut his profit margin in order to compete at the same price. Still another decade later the process is repeated, as a third new competitor is added. This one is able to produce goods at still lower prices and puts pressure on both predecessors.

In this way the combination of falling price and interest-rate levels and the series of depressions that have always accompanied the downswing of the long wave create a downward reinforcing spiral, which has historically lasted until the bottom of the deflationary phase, some three decades from the peak. The falling wholesale price level during this period also tends to aggravate the profit picture because the value of raw material, held for conversion into finished goods, declines. Such shrinkage in the values of these materials can only come out of profits. Profits are already under pressure from the competition of the lower-cost goods produced by the newly arrived competitors with their lower costs. Since overhead is fixed, that is, plant costs are sunk and money was borrowed at a fixed rate,† the profit squeezes often become intense.

Traditionally there have been three ways in which businessmen have sought to combat this squeeze:

---

†Bonds can of course be refunded, but only after a period of time (usually five years) and then only at a premium that tends to make the resultant cost of the refinanced bond higher than the cost of money for the new entrant.

reduce wages, combine to stabilize prices, or build new plants to produce profitably at lower prices. These three methods of dealing with the downward spiral have produced some of the most significant sociological and economic changes in American history. Let us examine them in detail. First there was the businessmen's need to offset the effects of the downward spiral through outright reductions in wages. This was particularly true of the thirty-year period of falling prices after the Civil War. America had developed into a sophisticated industrial society. Labor had more and more become a measurable unit of the costs of production in a complex and competitive capitalist system. Unlike the years following the War of 1812, America was no longer a nation of sedentary merchants and traders. Since products could not be easily differentiated from competing ones, pressures mounted, profits narrowed, and wages were cut.

It may be argued that the wage cuts were not really damaging since the price level was falling. There most likely were significant gains in real wages during the periods of prosperity in the years following the Civil War. However, no one living in any time in history likes to see his income reduced, and few are likely to accept such reductions cheerfully on the grounds that prices also are falling. Economists are fond of saying that workers have a "money illusion" when they speak of their attitude toward the constantly shifting relationship between wages and prices. But money illusion or no, to the worker facing a cut, fewer dollars look like more sacrifices. Labor's reaction was unionism.

Unionism in America goes back to the late eighteenth century, and over the years it has changed as the economy has changed. In the years before the Civil War, particularly in the period of falling prices between 1814 and 1844, union organization was chiefly among skilled groups. These groups produced carefully made, high-quality products. In the press of competition during that period of falling prices, entrepreneurs tried to substitute lower-cost labor and mass-production methods in the manufacture of their products. The marketing was done through sedentary merchants. Unionism made little truly significant progress in the early half of the century and was periodically wiped out during the serious depressions before 1844. From the 1844 price bottom until the Civil War period, unionism became somewhat stronger, with more continuity in its organization.

In 1866 the National Labor Union was formed. It was not successful. Its campaign for a reduction in the working hours of federal workers, for example, backfired when wages were reduced along with the number of working hours. While its ranks eventually reached half a million, the National Labor Union had none of the elements necessary to survive economic reversals and was wiped out by the depression of 1874–1879.

Other unions had sprung up around the country but most were insignificant. An exception was the Noble Order of the Knights of Labor, organized in Philadelphia in 1869. This union had one of the two vital elements of successful American unionism: it accepted anyone who was a worker. This concept was strong enough to hold the union together into the twentieth century. What the Knights of Labor gained from their single-union concept, they lost through their welfare unionism ideas, which concentrated on group benefits rather than individual wage increases. Furthermore their long-range approach, their dislike of strikes, and their failure to use direct political action eventually proved to be fatal errors of concept.

In the recovery years immediately following the depression of 1874–1879, however, American unionism found the two key ingredients for success: the concept of a single union for all workers and a business unionism approach. In 1881 the Federation of Organized Trades and Labor Unions was formed. This organization was the antecedent of the American Federation of Labor (AFL), which grew out of it in 1886 and which, of course, survives today.

The last really significant event in the early development of American unionism came in the years of declining prices and interest rates following the peak in 1920. The "euphoric 1920s" were not particularly good to unionism because there was still full employment. There was also little emotional upheaval of the kind that most Americans could identify with.† Times were good and both union and nonunion workers felt this. But the Great Depression of the 1930s changed things. A combination of the severe economic upheavals of the

---

†The IWW (International Workers of the World—also known as the Wobblies) was active during the 1920s, but radical unionism failed because it never really fitted the "American Dream."

early 1930s and the needs of unskilled workers, long neglected by the AFL (which maintained its craft-union attitude), led in 1935 to the formation of the Congress of Industrial Organizations.

Entrepreneurs attempted to cope with the fierce competition during periods of falling prices, particularly in the years following the Civil War, by combining into a few large companies and by fixing prices among those companies once the number of competitors had been reduced. It was a unique time, and it illustrates the influence of the downward reinforcing spiral better than either of the other two long-wave downswing periods because it offered exactly the right circumstances for business to organize for the restraint of trade on a large scale. The economy was not really developed enough by the time of the first downswing (between 1814 and 1844) for this to be an effective method of dealing with the grinding competition characteristic of downswings. By the time the third wave rolled around (after 1920) organization for the restraint of trade was illegal.

As a result the years of the 1870s and 1880s became the era of the magnate, the railroad baron, and the monopolist. It is not to excuse them or justify their deeds that we point out that such conduct might not have occurred in the same manner during a period of rising prices and interest rates. Beyond a doubt much of the activity was aimed at limiting the steady erosion of prices through the reduction of competition, just as the labor movement during the same period sought to reduce the pressure on wages by opposing immigration from certain parts of the world, particularly the Orient.

The tactics of the successful post-Civil War industrialists were not pleasant. They joined with some competitors and sought to destroy others. Many were destroyed. Markets were divided both geographically and on a percentage basis. Although shooting wars between rival factions sometimes took place, most industrialists were more genteel. In the steel business, for example, there was an annual dinner at which each producer was assigned a percentage of the total estimated production for the coming year. On the other hand John D. Rockefeller set out to create a monopoly in the oil business. Those who did not join him were doomed to fight and usually lost. The tendencies of industry to group together to limit or destroy competition, however, was due not to the avarice of selfish men but to two other factors: the relentless decline of prices and interest rates and the downward reinforcing spiral, which those falling rates and prices helped create because they gave the new entrant into an industry an absolute advantage over the established businessman. The downswing phase of the long wave, with its pressure on prices, provided exactly the right climate for business to seek relief through monopolistic combination.

The third way in which the entrepreneur sought to combat the effects of the downward reinforcing spiral was to take advantage of it. Andrew Carnegie is clearly the best example. Although playing the downward reinforcing spiral was far from being the sole reason for Carnegie's fantastic success, it was a significant factor

—a perfect long-range strategy. Carnegie was by no means the first American in the steel business, nor was he even one of the early entrants. He was not particularly knowledgeable about steelmaking, nor did he pioneer in the development of new techniques or the use of techniques that others developed. He did not, for example, use a Bessemer converter until nearly twenty years after it first appeared. Though he fitted the rags-to-riches pattern, he certainly was not a good fit for the Horatio Alger mold: he never worked particularly hard.

Yet Carnegie did have several extremely important talents. He picked good men to work for him and he paid well for results. He had the nerve to take substantial risks and seemed to have an extraordinary gift for picking the right ones. While he stayed away from pioneering, he was never afraid to spend money for a device or idea that would improve profits. He was supremely confident and also ruthless. With these attributes alone Carnegie could have become one of the important men in the steel industry. But Carnegie became one of the two or three most spectacularly successful entrepreneurs of all time. A major factor in his success was the way he used the downward reinforcing spiral to his own advantage, while it ruined many other men.

Carnegie's plan was basically simple. We do not know how he developed it but it required strong nerve to execute. During periods of prosperity, Carnegie accumulated cash and waited. When a depression arrived he would build, expand his capacity, and modernize. This is roughly opposite to the tactics of most entrepreneurs of his time and today, since it is easy to expand output in the face of rising demand but terrifying to do so in a depression. It must have taken great discipline and enormous courage and self-confidence to spend huge sums of money to add capacity with existing capacity standing idle. There were, of course, offsetting factors. One was that materials come at a bargain in a depression. Another was that he had planned ahead for the arrival of these depressions, so that when they arrived he was ready. Finally, there was Carnegie's insatiable competitive drive.

However he arrived at it, his strategy worked well. The first year that Carnegie was asked to the annual dinner at which the steel moguls divided the market for the year to come, he was assigned a modest share. He protested, an action that created an atmosphere of shocked disbelief. No one had ever dared talk back before. Full of his usual enormous self-confidence, he announced that he wanted a larger part of the market and intended to have it. When the other steelmakers regained their composure and told him to be satisfied with what he was given, Carnegie blithely announced that he could deliver finished steel to the user, at a profit, below the price at which the others could break even. It was not an idle threat. It was only a question of time before Carnegie dominated the industry.

The downward press of prices and interest rates and the resultant competitive squeeze caused other reactions in the industrial and transportation worlds during the post–Civil War years. The most important reaction was the relentless competition that attracted the attention of Wall Street. Too much competition was bad for profits, which was bad for shareholders, which was, in turn, very bad for the investment bankers. The leading investment banker of all time, J. Pierpont Morgan, became intensely concerned about the disorder in the transportation and industrial fields in the years following the Civil War. It appeared to him that the only way to bring order, to stop the falling prices and the intense, often ruinous, competition was to gain financial control of the leading entities in various industries. Morgan moved into the railroad industry first. He gradually brought an end to most of the rate wars, shut down or consolidated lines running in pointless competition to others, and created the first real stability that railroading had known. Later this was done in other industries.

Morgan was by no means powerful enough to do these things alone. He organized the efforts of many others, who formed an alliance to achieve a common goal. Those who joined Morgan were other investment bankers, commercial bankers, and the heads of various financial intermediaries, such as major life insurance companies. Morgan never dictated to these people. Instead of making demands, he had a genius for framing things in such a way that people realized it was mutually advantageous for them to do what Morgan wanted them to do. In this manner he was able to bring stability and profitability through the creation of voting trusts, interlocking directorates, and huge mergers.

The Sherman Anti-Trust Act of 1890 did not make Morgan's task easier, for it made any alliance for restraint of trade, or more exactly restraint of competition, illegal. Morgan was really in the middle. His motives were not to build great fortunes for the entrepreneurs who ran American industry at the expense of the workingman or the consumer. Nor were they solely directed toward the interests of the investors whom he represented. Morgan was chiefly interested in making the system of finance capitalism work well. This required that competition did not become ruinous and that the investor was rewarded. A check on competition did not work to the detriment of the workingman. If it functioned properly there would be less pressure on wages, fuller employment, and greater economic stability. J. Pierpont Morgan was not what many people imagine him to be. He never operated solely or even primarily for profit. He worked for order in a system that would break down without order and that was, through the relentless grinding of competition, being threatened with collapse. Today Morgan's actions would be in violation of the antitrust laws. But before those laws and before the days of a strong central government, Morgan held things together when there was little else. He had little sense of social responsibility as we know it today because he never concerned himself with the plight of the individual. But he was intensely concerned with the American capitalist system itself, upon which every man depended. Many of his ideas have become public policy. For example, the federal government regulates certain basic industries and even, in the case of utilities, grants its permission for legal monopolies.

Like many a period whose legend lives far beyond

itself, the years of laissez-faire capitalism, which were confined chiefly to the thirty-year downswing in prices and interest rates following the Civil War, were relatively short-lived. While the antitrust laws were gradually strengthened, the expanding prosperity of the years after the 1896 price bottom shifted the emphasis from cost reduction to innovation and volume expansion in industry. By the time the downswing that began in 1920 became a problem to business, that is, after 1929, the emphasis had shifted from the problems of destructive competition toward those of insufficient demand and, to some extent, the influence of foreign competition.

The downswing of the first long wave halted in 1844 and the downswing of the second in 1896. The downswing phase of the third great wave was obliterated after the 1930s by the beginning of World War II. At the end of the 1930s, however, the long wave appeared to have been at exactly the same point in its development as it was in the two previous downswings that had been in progress for a comparable period of time.

While secondary postwar depressions appear to be the most devastating for the economy because of their severity and protracted life, the last years of the downswing have also been among the most gloomy of the wave. It was not for nothing that the bottom of the first wave, for example, was referred to as the "Hungry Forties." The entire period, a total of sixty-four months from 1839 through 1843, was one of serious economic depression. Similarly the last years of the second downswing saw the nation foundering in depression for most of the forty-six months prior to the 1896 bottom.

In the most recent downswing, which began in 1920, the nation was spared a third decade of decline (which would have encompassed the 1940s) by the huge economic stimulus of World War II. The primary postwar recession of 1920, the secondary one of 1929, and the tertiary one of 1937 were behind us, but the final bottoming out was yet to come. While the policies of Franklin Roosevelt's New Deal were in full swing during his second term, which began in 1936, the 1937 "submerged" peak dealt a sharp blow to the confidence that had been so nearly restored. The sudden stock-market collapse of February 1937, which saw prices drop more than 40 percent from a post-1929-crash recovery high, was a frightening experience when the memory of the great crash was so close at hand. It was partly because of this that there was not unbridled optimism in the years following World War II.

When the stock market hit its next low in May 1942 (lower than the 1938 low), few people saw the moment as one of great opportunity. While it is true that the wartime climate was not one that encouraged speculation in common stocks, the two depressions of the 1930s must also have been influential. It was possible to be bullish about the future in the early 1940s, but for many it was simply easier to look back to the turmoil, the economic disaster, the frightening unemployment, and be cautious or flatly pessimistic in one's forecast than it was to look ahead to the trillion-dollar-economy. For the few who did, however, the rewards were great. From the 1942 low, the stock market advanced 300 percent in the next ten years alone. The economy never did turn down because by the time the massive boost from World War II had been absorbed, the long wave had run its course. From the late 1940s on, the upswing was in full force.

CHAPTER 4
THE UPSWINGS

The United States has been in an upswing for more than twenty years, but most Americans probably never considered these years to be only one part of a long economic wave. They accepted the situation as the result of good economic management, the way things were, are, and will be, because they believed that we now know how to manage the economy.

Unfortunately most Americans were wrong. The upswing part of the long wave, which created the prosperity after World War II that we have now accepted as our birthright, is over. The memories, however, are worth keeping. The period from 1950 to 1970 displayed all the characteristics of every upswing in American history.

Each of the two-decade periods of upswing has been

similar, not just in terms of wages, prices, and business conditions, but in the way people behaved. Kondratieff said that the period of upswing was one of rising tensions, a time of wars and revolution. Let us see how this concept stands up, using the three periods of upswing for which we were able to obtain accurate records—the two decades from 1844 through the Civil War, the two decades from 1896 through World War I, and the two decades from about 1950 to the present.

In our discussion of the periodicity of wars, we showed that the predictable wars occurred just *after* the troughs in prices (trough wars) and just before the peaks (peak wars). Technically, therefore, both kinds of wars occur in the upswing. There is, however, a vast difference between the peak and trough wars. The peak wars (the War of 1812, the Civil War, World War I, and the Vietnam War) generated strong emotions in the United States, whereas the trough wars (the Mexican, Spanish-American, and Korean wars) were taken in stride. This is a reflection of the emotional climate created by the rising tide of prosperity. At the beginning of the upswing, the public is still in the relatively calm state characteristic of the decline, particularly the end of the decline. Intermittent periods of economic depression force people to be predominantly concerned with their own well-being and less interested in international affairs and military crusades. The Civil War, World War I, and the Vietnam War, in particular, started with this crusader flavor. But unlike the trough wars, which never seemed to get so far out of hand, these peak wars lost public support as they became larger, difficult to fight, and costly to win.

People seem unable to cope with the mounting complications of life as the long-wave peak approaches; they have no stamina for keeping up with an accelerating rate of change. The Vietnam years brought the kind of public discontent, eventually reflected in public disorder, that is typical. Resistance to the wars or the political system responsible for them has always occurred during the peak wars, not the trough wars.

In July 1863, during the Civil War, bloody draft riots erupted in New York City. As many as 50,000 people roamed the streets for four days, burning, looting, and killing Negroes. At the same time there was political resistance to Lincoln and to the Union's military effort by an organization, composed mostly of northern Democrats, dubbed the Copperheads. After a while, of course, anyone who openly opposed the Lincoln administration was called a Copperhead. Similarly, in World War I, the hostilities started as a crusade but the public became progressively disillusioned. The May Day riots in 1919 were the culmination of this discontent and were both against the war and against the capitalist establishment. A series of terrorist bombings also occurred. The events surrounding the Vietnam War are more familiar and need not be reexamined at this point, except to show them to be part of a syndrome that can be expected during a long-wave upswing.

The tensions, frustrations, and excitement associated with the upswing do not, of course, begin immediately after prices reach the bottom of their thirty-year decline. The final depression of the downswing has always been a long and dismal period. When it ends, the initial reaction is one of cautious relief. There is little evidence that a permanent change has occurred, for the period resembles the earlier recoveries from the recent and less severe recessions. That there will, in fact, be no serious downturns again for twenty years is not evident to those entering an upswing. The war that follows the trough diverts attention from the economy, at least briefly. A mild upswing recession eventually washes over the nation, but the effects are small compared to recessions during the downswing. As the years pass, the public's confidence and resources build. What had been inward-turning against the cold blast of the deflation-depression syndrome and the downward reinforcing spiral gradually relaxes and begins to open, to turn outward. As things heat up and expand, the inflation-prosperity syndrome takes over. Like the spiral created by the decline of prices and interest rates, there is a spiral created by their upward bias.

The upward reinforcing spiral has the same attributes as the one that operates downward, except that it operates in the opposite direction. As a result those who are to benefit from it must be "on stream" as early in the game as possible. Obviously, building one's plant early in the upward swing, before the prices of labor, material, and land rise, and borrowing money at low rates of interest can mean high profits and low overhead. In addition, as the price of raw materials keeps rising, so do profits for those who bought low, because most accounting systems generally consider the increased value of raw materials as profits. Moreover, as these raw materials move through the plant, prices for finished goods are also rising and the manufacturer can charge more while most of his costs remain stable. Wages and taxes do rise, but the rise in prices is more than able to offset this. As we pointed out earlier, the workingman has what economists call a money illusion —he is far happier with rising prices and rising wages than with falling ones. The net result is that during the upswing the optimists, the chance-takers win. They might have been forced to the wall had they used the same tactics during the downswing. Those who get leveraged up early, borrowing large sums to buy income-producing properties, are generally able to amass considerable fortunes, while the cautious saver sits by, expecting a rebirth of the deflation. By the time the general public becomes convinced that the downswing is not likely to reappear, the economy is well into the upswing years. Savings, partially eaten by inflation, have lost power while the borrowers of those savings have actually multiplied their wealth. Suddenly inflation, not the prospect of recurring deflation, becomes the popularly recognized villain, and those whose fathers may have followed the paths of frugality find that the old values are no longer the ones that work.

Nothing exemplifies the unconscious use of the upward reinforcing spiral better than real estate. Real estate speculators, of course, differ from most of us. Everything they see holds the potential of earning them a million dollars. The beginning of the long-wave upswing is the ideal time for this kind of outlook and for speculation in real estate. Even more than the manufacturer, the real estate speculator is aided by rising prices and interest rates.† The raw material of real estate is land, and this is perhaps the most important factor in profits. It is so important, in fact, that many developers, particularly those developing recreational properties, plan to make their money on the land. They provide the buildings mostly to create a salable package. Nothing fluctuates in price so greatly as land. When the economy is down, really down, undeveloped land sinks to incredible levels. When the prospect that something will be built on it is revived, the price doubles, triples, and quadruples. For the real estate speculator, the profits under such conditions can be staggering.

Land booms have occurred on and off in the United States and most have, like economic musical chairs, left some of the participants standing in the cold. Prosperous times and the same tireless land speculators' slogan —"there'll never be any more land than there is right now"—have always been the two vital ingredients. A quick land boom can occur in a brief period of prosperity, either in the long-wave upswing or downswing; but it is the long upswing, not the quick boom, that the real estate investor can best use. Watching others make money by riding the upward reinforcing spiral, while their assets sit in the form of savings, eventually becomes too much for some people, but too late.

---

†Eventually, however, those same prices and interest rates place limits on his expansionary schemes.

Speculations like the Florida land boom of the 1920s, in which thousands of ordinary people invested heavily in Sunshine State properties, frequently result after the real gains have been made by professionals.

Perhaps the most prominent example of an entrepreneur whose tactics were well suited to operating an industrial organization during the upswing of the long wave was Henry Ford. He launched his first automobile company in 1899, just three years after the long-wave price bottom.† Although he was a gifted man, his tactics probably would have been far less successful in a period of declining prices; his approach was geared to an economy with rapidly expanding demand, and he paid little heed to cost control. Ford actually was not responsible for many of the things that he is generally believed to have developed. For example, the assembly line was conceived by R. E. Olds, father of the Oldsmobile. Rather, Ford brilliantly combined techniques developed by others.

The most important factor in Ford's success, however, was his accurate assessment of the potential market represented by the man in the street. During the period of expanding prosperity prior to World War I, Ford endeavored to produce a car at a price the man in the street could afford. He identified the market first and then developed the techniques that brought the price down (relative to the rising price-wave level) to

---

†The company failed. The second company, which survives today, was founded in 1903 with $28,000. The Ford Motor Company has never raised additional capital from outside sources.

within reach of the man in the street. Ford did not set out to build a mass-production product, but rather a product that only mass production could provide at the desired price. Without the expanding prosperity that the upswing of the wave gave to the man in the street, Ford would not have prospered. A period of protracted depression during his early years might have also been disastrous. As it was, the recession of 1920–1921, the first of the long-wave downswing, caught him with heavy inventories of finished cars. Ford has been accused of pushing off large numbers of cars on his dealers during this period to avoid the intense financial pressure of the tight money squeeze in which the Federal Reserve System had placed the economy. As we mentioned earlier, Ford's chief competitor, Will Durant of General Motors, experienced the same pressure and was forced to seek help from the Du Pont family in exchange for about 25-percent ownership of GM.

There seems to be no rational basis for the upswing of the long wave any more than there is for the downswing. The upswing lasts about two decades rather than three. As we will show in detail later, however, the first decade of the downswing years is quite unique in that it is a time of near-euphoric prosperity and seems to contain none of the ills of the two-decade period of prosperity that precedes it. The periodicity of the entire wave is puzzling. It is not hard to see why, through a kind of economic inertia, things might continue in one direction for some time. But what makes them reverse?

Even more difficult to understand is why the reversal should come at a predictable time.

But the reversals of trend do come, and between them some very definite things occur at predictable places in the wave. Let us look specifically at some of the things that happen during the upswing years. First, there is the action of wholesale commodity prices. On a scale where 1957–1959 prices equal 100, the prices at the various peaks and troughs (through the 1920 peak) were as follows:

1814	62.3	(peak)
1843	25.4	(trough)
1864	74.7	(peak)
1896	25.4	(trough)
1920	84.5	(peak)

From 1920 on, prices declined for two decades; World War II obliterated the price decline in its final decade. Before the war the downward trend was still operating; without the stimulant of war, the economy would probably have moved into a bottoming depression in the late 1940s.

Using the same scale as above (1957–1959 = 100), the action of prices from the 1920 peak forward was (showing depression and recovery fluctuations):

1920	84.5	(year average)
1929	52.1	(year average)
1932	35.6	(year average)
1933	32.7	(February)
1937	48.2	(April and July)
1939	41.0	(August)

It may be seen that prices were lower in 1929 than in 1920 (most of this developed in 1921) and still lower in 1932 and 1933. (The actual low point of the depression occurred in February 1933, but prices were lower on the average in 1932 than in 1933.) The recovery lasted until 1937, when the third in a series of post–World War I depressions began. By August 1939 prices still had not recovered to the 1937 level, but with the advent of World War II, prices started to be influenced by heavy armament expenditures. The trend of prices during the two decades from 1950 to 1970, which were the *predicted* years of price upswing, was, as everyone knows, up.

Data on interest rates match these data on prices, although there is about a two-year lag at some peaks and troughs. We have seen how interest rates play an important role in both the upward and downward reinforcing spirals. Despite Shakespeare's advice that one should "neither a borrower nor a lender be," the long-wave actions of interest rates indicate that such decisions are a matter of timing. Those who lend at peaks and borrow at troughs do very nicely.

The severity of economic downturns is significantly less during the years of rising prices and interest rates than during the long-wave decline. In addition, such setbacks in the economy do not last nearly as long, on the average, as the depressions that occur in the downswing. One indication of the relative severity of downturns is that fact that the word *depression* has not been used since the 1930s. The recessions that have occurred since the upswing began two decades ago may have been softened by the so-called built-in stabilizers, like unemployment compensation and deficit spending, but the downturns that occurred in the upswing phases of other waves were equally mild and short-lived.

For example, in the downswing years from the 1814 to the 1843 price bottom, there were four depressions, while there were only two from 1844 through 1864. Three out of four of these downswing depressions were of greater severity than the two of the upswing years. Three out of four (not the same three) were also longer. The differences in length were particularly significant: the longest depression in the downswing ran nearly three times as long as the longest of the upswing.

Similar comparisons are seen in the three decades of declining prices and interest rates from the Civil War to the 1896 bottom and in the upswing years from 1896 to 1920. In this wave, the downswing depressions were on the average only slightly more severe than those of the upswing, but they were exceptionally protracted. The secondary post–Civil War depression, which was the longest in American history, gripped the nation for seventy months, whereas two others ran thirty-one and forty-six months. Only the primary post-peak-war depression was short (eleven months), as most of these tend to be. The depressed periods of the upswing years were by contrast much shorter, ranging from fourteen to twenty months.

The downswing of the third wave started off with a sharp jolt, with the primary post–World War I depression running for twenty-three months and reaching a greater degree of severity than any depression prior to that time. This was followed by the Great Depression of the 1930s, when the contraction phase alone began about two months before the stock-market crash and ran for forty-three months.

The recessions of the long-wave upswing from 1950 to 1970 have not only been significantly milder and shorter than those of past downswings, but milder and shorter than those of past upswings too. There is no doubt that the built-in stabilizers have had a role in this. So has the Federal Reserve System. It must be remembered that this is the first complete long-wave upswing during which the "Fed" has operated. It was not created until 1913, when the previous upswing was two-thirds over. Hence it never really had a chance to operate as a counterbalance against the forces of a recession until the downturn of 1920–1921, the primary post–World War I recession when, interestingly enough, the "Fed" did exactly the wrong thing. It happened like this.

At the beginning of the 1920s the country was experiencing the severe inflation that is part of the peak-war syndrome. World War I was over but successive waves of price increases were still washing the economy. In June 1920 the economy finally began to turn down, yet the Federal Reserve System continued to apply pressure to the money market until late 1921. According to economist Milton Friedman, the money supply—one measure of such pressure—dwindled 8.2 percent between March 1920 and January 1922. This unfortunate error seriously aggravated the recession. Wholesale prices fell over 50 percent, and unemployment reached nearly 12 percent. The Federal Reserve System had simply misread the signs: acting as the nation's central bank, accustomed to leaning into the wind during the final phase of the long-term upswing, it had suddenly come face to face with the downturn.

The 1970–1971 recession was the primary one of the next long-wave downswing. It was not, in the strict sense of the word, a postwar recession because the war was still on. But the recession was clearly part of the inflationary peak syndrome, and the roots of its causes were the same ones that caused every other primary post-peak-war recession. This time, however, while the Federal Reserve System applied pressure to the economy prior to this recession, just as it applied it prior to the 1920–1921 downturn, it was careful to ease again once the dip was under way. But the 1970–1971 downturn, which was clearly the most severe since the 1930s, was no real test. Whether or not the powers of the Federal Reserve System can really prevent a depression will not be put to a real test until the 1980s. That test was failed in the 1930s, but not because of errors by the "Fed." When we say that the system's efforts can stay a major downswing-phase depression, we are vastly overrating its powers. The recessions of the past two decades, when they proved to be only mild ones, served to reinforce this misconception.

Another phenomenon of the upswing—as with the downswing—is that the trend shapes opinion to conform to it. If business is down, everyone says it is down and is going to stay down. When it is up, everyone says prosperity will never end.

One illustration of how the long trend shapes opinion and how events seem to fit in is the Full Employment Act of 1945. In America, if you want to stop something, you pass a law. After the experience of the 1930s, the public wanted to put a stop to what was, but was not recognized as, the long-wave downswing. Shaken by the years of deflation and business depression, it was felt that unless some basis of permanent government intervention was established the nation would slide back into the downtrend once the stimulus of wartime spending disappeared. This would have been an accurate hypothesis had not the three decades of deflation been coming to an end. However, Kondratieff's long-wave theory had little impact on the contemporary economic thinking of the day, despite the extensive works that Joseph Schumpeter and others had published on the subject in the late 1930s. To avoid the specter of another bout with intense deflation, unemployment, and business depression, Senator James E. Murray of Montana introduced a bill in January 1945 to assure every

American "able and willing to work" not the privilege but the "the right" to employment. The dark days of the past had changed the attitude about unemployment, as well as the economics of combating it.

It was not the concept of a managed economy, the automatic stabilizers created under the Full Employment Act of 1945 or the Federal Reserve System that fueled the prosperity we have enjoyed during these past two decades. The public, however, now believes that because of these things prosperity is here to stay. The 1970s will further entrench these beliefs, and by the 1980s the probability of a major economic downturn will generally be considered to be near zero. The trend will have again shaped opinion, this time toward a belief in perpetual prosperity. The arsenal of economic weapons will perhaps be more valuable as a rationale for perpetual prosperity than it will be as a cure for deflation when its time finally comes.

As the uptrend shapes public opinion to the position that the last serious downturn is over and that the future is a continuum of prosperity, other attitudinal changes take place. With the rising tide of prosperity there is a rise in expectations. Whereas people had been reasonably acquiescent toward their economic lot in the early years of the upturn, they become increasingly discontented as the general level of prosperity rises. The initial relief from the downward pressures gives way to a dissatisfaction with the upward ones. Kondratieff blamed the frequency of wars and revolutions during the upswing on the rising tensions of the period of prosperity. Tensions do build and they are a significant

factor, particularly in the explosive incidents characteristic of the long-wave peaks. However, expectations are
another factor that perhaps contribute to the building
of prosperity-borne tension or perhaps exert a separate
and distinct influence themselves. In either case the
rising tide of prosperity creates rising expectations, and
since the economy cannot possibly deliver on these expectations as quickly as they rise, a frustration with the
state of things, with the very progress toward fulfill-
ment of human needs and desires, is created.

In societies where frustrations can be vented and
where the general level of material possessions and income are high enough, the move toward violent revolution is confined to a small and eventually unsuccessful
minority. We see this in America of the late 1960s and
early 1970s, with the conviction, by a vociferous few
hard-liners, that the society must be torn down and
remade.

Such people do contribute to lasting change, of
course, for their more moderate proposals are eventually incorporated into national policy. But it is a very
difficult thing to make a revolution. It takes more than
just the normal frustrations and discontent brought
about by unfilled expectations during the upswing of
prosperity. If a revolution were to succeed, it needs a
mass of people who are, by and large, left disenfranchised while a few prosper. Radical politics and the
message of destroy and rebuild have never succeeded in
America because there have never been enough people
truly left out of the benefits of an expanding prosperity.
America has simply been too prosperous, and each man

has amassed too much to throw it all away. A man with something to lose makes a poor revolutionary.

Many events and political movements during the years of upswing and rising prosperity are due solely to that prosperity and the mood it creates. This is true, for example, in the area of foreign trade. Throughout American history, the nation's attitude about free trade versus trade barriers (tariffs and quotas) has varied with the long-wave trend. As a rule of thumb, if wholesale commodity prices and interest rates were rising, America moved toward freer trade; when the nation was in the downswing, public sentiment swung toward restriction. This is not to imply that legislation was passed instantly, that the day after the peak was reached massive barriers were thrown up, or that after the trough all tariffs were lowered to zero. But without exception every constructive piece of free-trade legislation was passed between 1843 and the Civil War, between 1896 and World War I, or in the last two decades.† Similarly in the years after the peaks, when declining prices activated the downward reinforcing spiral, when both business and labor felt the pinch, public attitudes swung toward restrictive imports.

The protectionist case for restricting trade is and always has been without merit, and there are few if any economists who would argue differently. As Paul Samuelson said recently in opposition to a present-day shoe and textile import quota bill: "I would say that this is

---

†There were tariff reductions during downswings, often because of demands from agricultural states, but they could hardly be called free trade measures.

one of the least controversial areas of economic analysis. In 1930, all the economists warned against the high Smoot-Hawley tariff. They warned about the dire consequences to our welfare, to the world welfare. . . . alas, they were right. Now to a man they all agree. When Milton Friedman and I are on the same side, it's a pretty strong case." The Smoot-Hawley tariff to which Samuelson referred is but one example of the protective posture of the downswing years. There are many others.

In the years of falling prices and interest rates after the War of 1812, tariffs were high. Wartime tariffs were extended by the tariff of 1816, raised by the tariff of 1824 (to 33⅓ percent), and raised again by the 1828 "tariff of abominations" (to 41 percent). After this point tariffs were reduced somewhat, having received heavy pressure from the South (South Carolina threatened secession) in 1832 and again in 1833. The 1833 tariff was referred to as the "compromise tariff." Sentiment remained strongly protectionist, however, and as prices continued to fall tariffs were again increased in 1841 over the stiff opposition of the South, led by John C. Calhoun. Calhoun maintained that the increase violated the compromise of 1833. When prices and interest rates began to rise again after 1843, a free-trade spirit swept through the nation. The rising economic level instilled new confidence in the nation's attitude toward competition, and when the grinding pressure of the downward reinforcing spiral gave way to the lift of the upward one, trade barriers began to fall. The problems of falling prices had become ones of rising prices, and the public was ready to accept the challenge and the benefits of freer trade.

The Walker tariff of 1846 was a concise expression of the free-trade point of view and a milestone in American tariff legislation. Nothing like it was to be seen again until the next upswing of the long wave, in 1913. The Walker tariff did not eliminate tariffs, but the sentiment behind it was to move the nation toward freer trade and away from protectionism. Tariffs were again reduced in 1857. This was more of a victory for the manufacturers of the North, because the reductions were greatest on raw materials, than for the South and West, which also backed it.

With the coming of the Civil War, tariffs were raised once again. The Morrill Tariff Act moved the levels back to where they had been prior to the reductions of 1857. It was framed as a revenue measure to meet federal deficits, which were mounting in the years *prior* to the secession of the South. It was not designed to be a barrier to imports, but it did begin to make imported goods more expensive. The protectionists followed up later. As it developed, the Morrill bill was passed just days before Lincoln took office, and it became the vehicle that Salmon P. Chase, Lincoln's secretary of the treasury, hoped would provide him with badly needed revenues.

In the years following the Civil War, the protectionists were able to resist efforts by the free traders to have the tariffs imposed during the war removed. The years of depression that the nation experienced from 1874–1879 did not help the free-trade cause. However, as business began to recover late in the 1870s, pressure began to mount. As in the first half of the century, agitation for lower duties came particularly from the agricultural blocks in the South and West. President Chester Arthur, a strong protectionist, would probably not have yielded on the subject except for one common characteristic of the downswing phase: the federal government was running budgetary surpluses. Had these surpluses not been so large and consistent (the government ran a surplus every year from 1866 through 1893), it might have been impossible to force the President to face heavy protectionist sentiment. Tariffs, however, were then a significant factor in federal revenues and, remarkable as it sounds, the nation was being embarrassed by having too much money and nothing to do with it.

The largest of the twenty-eight consecutive federal surpluses was run in 1882. This in effect forced President Arthur's hand. A commission that was appointed made recommendations to Congress, which were ignored, for what became the tariff of 1883. By one of those incredible masterpieces of legislative maneuver, of which only the U.S. Congress and perhaps a scant handful of other legislative bodies are capable, rates on various commodities were only shuffled around and the average level of tariffs was actually raised.

The next revision in the tariff laws came in 1890. Prices and interest rates were by this time in their third decade of decline from their Civil War peak, and the protectionists were in full gallop. Though the federal surpluses had continued uninterrupted, the protectionists were determined to increase tariffs. President Benjamin Harrison, who was a protectionist, was pledged to do what seemed to be two mutually exclusive things: raise tariffs and lower federal revenues. But the protectionists showed considerable imagination in implementing these policies. The duty on sugar imports, which equaled more than half of the federal surplus, was eliminated. At the same time domestic producers were paid a subsidy. This had the effect of keeping the imported sugar at a disadvantage in the marketplace without collecting unneeded revenues. These measures were incorporated into the McKinley tariff of 1890, which was through-and-through a protectionist document.

The last years of the downswing, which were ones of bitter depression, began in the 1890s. While public sentiment had started to show the first stirrings toward freer trade in these years as the long-wave bottom was nearing, the protectionists were still in control of the Congress. The Wilson tariff was drafted in 1894 in response to the growing public dissatisfaction with the McKinley tariff. But the protectionist opposition managed to add over 600 amendments to the bill, which effectively nullified its free-trade reform. The parting shot of the protectionists was fired in 1897 with the Dingley tariff. The depression, which had begun in 1893, the final bottoming one of the long-wave downswing, had ended the previous year. The free-trade spirit, which rises with the shift to rising prices and interest rates, was not yet really on the march. The Dingley tariff raised the average level of import duties to 52 percent. This was the highest that tariffs had ever been.

It took another ten years of rising prices for public sentiment to build to a point at which the protectionists were outnumbered and the free traders could gain the upper hand. This became apparent at the Republican Convention of 1908, when the party drafted a platform that did not express the protectionist point of view. The next year the Payne bill to reduce import duties was introduced in Congress. The bill passed the House but the forces of protectionism, which by this time represented only a minority of the population, were still a majority in the Senate. The bill was amended over 800 times and reduced from a strong free-trade measure to a minor reform. The resultant act was the Payne-Aldrich tariff of 1909.

By 1913 the protectionists could no longer block the progress of the free traders and the majority of the nation they represented. The years of rising prices had generated public discontent with the tariff barriers because the man in the street now blamed the continued rise of prices on the protection of American industry from foreign competitors. Though the attempt to reduce the high tariff wall had failed in 1909, with the protectionist-dominated Senate's counterattack on the Aldrich reform, the trade-barrier advocates were on the run after the election of Woodrow Wilson. The Underwood bill was nothing less than a sweeping reform of tariff rates. As with predecessor reforms, the bill passed the House with ease, and with the powerful backing that Wilson gave it, it also passed the Senate, virtually intact. The Underwood tariff in effect rolled rates back to where they had been in 1857, during the previous period of rising prices and interest rates that had ended in 1865. Like the tariff of 1857, this was the last attempt at a reduction during the upswing. The measure was doomed to be repealed once the protectionist sentiment, born in the next downswing, began to grow in the years following the 1920 long-wave peak.

In the early 1920s America turned toward an isolationism and a nationalism that was to set the tone for nearly two decades. The mood of economic nationalism in 1922, when the Fordney-McCumber tariff was enacted, was not unlike the very similar situation that prevailed at the time the tariff of 1816 was passed. The wartime inflationary peak syndrome had given way to the plateau decade of mild deflation and the continued momentum of prosperity. Despite the Fordney-McCumber tariff, American exports remained high. It might have been expected that increasing tariffs after World War I would create war reparations payment difficulties in Europe or at least slow its ability to buy our export commodities. This was not the case because America was also exporting capital in the form of huge foreign loans. This flow of funds into Europe, which reached nearly $1 billion per year, enabled European countries to make large purchases despite the tariff wall.

As the long-wave downswing progressed and the momentum of prosperity faded, strength built in the protectionist camp. In June 1930, eight months after the great stock-market crash of the previous year, Senator Smoot of Utah joined Representative Hawley of Oregon to produce a bill that established the highest import duties in American history. No single act of protectionism could have been more damaging or more ill timed. The Smoot-Hawley tariff made trade with America impossibly difficult. Together with the contraction of loans to European buyers of American goods, this act comprised a one-two punch with which the wobbly economy was ill equipped to deal. For, as the Great Depression intensified, trade was already falling off.

The policies of Franklin Roosevelt, though differing little in the initial years from those of the Republican administration and their embrace of the protectionist doctrine, gradually swung toward tariff reform. Because Smoot-Hawley had been such a clear disaster, because the nation was in such desperate straits, and most important because the Roosevelt administration had a clear mandate from the American people to change what it deemed necessary to change, it was possible for the new administration to overcome the protectionists. Roosevelt's approach was not exactly free trade; what he asked for and got was the authority to enter into *reciprocal* trade agreements. This approach of "you lower yours and I'll lower mine," while not actually free trade, was not deliberately restrictive. Unlike the free-trade years, when an America confident of its ability to compete with all comers simply lowered its duties across-the-board, these agreements were selective. They did work, however.

In the two decades of rising prosperity just past, the free-trade question first rose in the 1950s and eventually found full expression in John F. Kennedy's round of tariff reductions of the early 1960s. Particularly in the mid and latter 1960s, a combination of the fear that inflation would become an unmanageable danger and the almost overwhelming confidence in America's ability to compete kept the free-trade spirit at the forefront of trade policy. With the advent of the peak-war syndrome and the primary recession of the long-wave downswing, the situation began to reverse quickly. The stirrings of the protectionists, almost dormant for many years, were again heard in 1970. This time protectionism began with the proposal of quotas for shoes and textiles. But quotas are even more damaging than simple tariffs because they offer inefficient industries absolute shelter no matter how bad they get. In this, their first battle, the protectionists went down to defeat, as the quotas they wanted were denied. But they will be back and next time will probably win.

It may be seen from the history of tariff legislation that, when prices and interest rates were periodically in a three-decade period of decline, protectionists got and kept the upper hand and only when the strong forces of upswing made it overwhelmingly obvious that trade restrictions were unnecessary were tariffs and duties removed. The fact that the absurdity of trade barriers periodically forced some reforms is of little consolation. It takes the disaster of a Smoot-Hawley to precipitate a reform in the downswing. Then, at the long-wave peak, the protectionists are back with the same fallacious arguments, ready to close down trade once again.

CHAPTER 5

THE FEDERAL BUDGET

During the administration of John F. Kennedy, the President and his economic advisors tried to explain Keynesian economics to the public, justifying budget deficits as a necessary evil during periods of economic slack. Deficit spending would end, they promised, as soon as the economy regained its health. But the deficits did not end. Although the gross national product, standard barometer of economic conditions, rose close to the trillion-dollar mark, red ink still marked the federal ledgers. Even under such a professed conservative as Richard Nixon, federal spending continued to exceed revenues.

The reason was not bad management or willful manipulation. It was only another characteristic of the

Kondratieff wave, for federal spending and federal budgets follow the long wave. The past two decades were no exception; the seventies will be no different. Here is what has happened.

In the periods of rapid economic expansion, when prices and interest rates were rising, the government also took an expansionist stance and spent freely. During the downtrend, however, when business was having a tougher time, the government reflected the national attitude of caution. This is reflected in the balance of federal budgets. In the decade following a peak of prices and interest rates, the federal budget shows surpluses nearly every year. As the downswing continues, there are fewer surpluses in each decade. When the upswing begins during the fourth decade after the preceding peak, there are even fewer years of surplus; and in the fifth decade it balances almost not at all. We have just experienced the fourth and fifth decades of the long wave, and we are about to enter the first decade of the next wave.

The 1970s should, therefore, bring what conservatives are fond of calling "a return to fiscal sanity." It will not, however, be the result of a change of attitude on the part of the federal government so much as a change of circumstances under which it must operate. It will not be the determination to reduce federal expenditures that will create surpluses, it will be the peaking of the long wave.

At the long-wave peak, two things happen that turn a string of deficits into a string of surpluses. First, after years of mounting tensions and rising expectations that culminate during and just after the wave peak, the nation shifts away from the expansionist, internationalist, promilitary stance of the upswing and starts demanding that the government spend more conservatively. Second, as military expenditures are reduced with the termination of the peak war, prices stop rising and industry is no longer asked to produce beyond its most efficient capacity. The gross national product may grow at a slower rate or may even fall slightly during the recession following the price peak, but once the war is over expenditures tend to fall even more rapidly, surpluses pile up, and the public presses for tax reductions. Under the unique circumstances of the first decade after the peak (relatively high prosperity and stable or slightly falling prices), tax reductions tend to *increase* revenues because they stimulate the economy, which, relieved of the demands of the military, has room to be stimulated. Then taxes are reduced again and surpluses continue. The mild deflationary bias given the economy by the surpluses helps reduce the cost of government to a level below what it would be if prices were rising.

The 1970s, therefore, will be characterized by federal expenditures reduced in relation to the gross national product, federal surpluses, stable prices or mild deflation, high prosperity, and no inflation. It will be a time when material wants, long denied by years of war and inflation, will be filled—years when American industry will produce goods to fill those needs rather than produce consumables for war. There will, of course, still be those in want, and the federal government will increasingly come to their aid; but it will not produce deficits.

The pattern of federal budget deficits and surpluses closely corresponds to the ebb and flow of the long wave. Until the middle 1930s no attempt was ever made to soften economic reversals with federal spending. On the contrary depressions were always met with cries for reduced spending, which, although aimed at aiding economic recovery, was precisely the opposite of what should have been done.

To see the relationship of the federal budget to the long wave, we should look at the record of deficits and surpluses. We will examine five decades per wave, but because each wave was, in fact, slightly longer than fifty years (averaging about fifty-two years) and because no two waves were of *exactly* the same length, the fifteen decades examined must be fitted into three waves that actually covered a period of about 156 years. This does not distort the results. Any other fitting would produce approximately the same conclusions. The tallies are as follows:

First Decade		*Deficit years*	*Surplus years*
FIRST WAVE	1816–1825	3	7
SECOND WAVE	1866–1875	0	10
THIRD WAVE	1920–1929	0	10
	TOTAL	3	27

Second Decade		*Deficit Years*	*Surplus Years*
FIRST WAVE	1826–1835	0	10
SECOND WAVE	1876–1885	0	10
THIRD WAVE	1930–1939	9	1
	TOTAL	9	21

Third Decade

FIRST WAVE	1836–1845	6	4
SECOND WAVE	1886–1895	2	8
THIRD WAVE	1940–1949	8	2
	TOTAL	16	14

Fourth Decade

FIRST WAVE	1846–1855	3	7
SECOND WAVE	1896–1905	6	4
THIRD WAVE	1950–1959	7	3
	TOTAL	16	14

Fifth Decade

FIRST WAVE	1856–1865	8	2
SECOND WAVE	1906–1915	6	4
THIRD WAVE	1960–1969	9	1
	TOTAL	23	7

It may be seen at a glance that the first decades immediately following the long-wave peaks have almost always been characterized by more surpluses than deficits and that the ratio shifts until, during the last decade of each wave, there are far more deficits than surpluses. The years between form an even progression from one state to the other. The reasons for this shift are not difficult to understand if we understand the long wave and its influence on the economy.

In the first decade after the peak a large revenue-gathering system, still geared to its role in wartime finance, gathers more money than is needed from the still prosperous economy, while military appropriations are cut sharply and the general price level falls or remains stable. In the second decade, the secondary post-war depression hits. A characteristic of this depression is that it is usually severe and always drawn out. During the first two decades of the first two waves, the government was able to reduce expenditures as revenues fell. In the third decades of those two waves deficits were, however, run reluctantly and only when the government was unable to reduce expenditures quickly or far enough. But during the third wave—from the middle 1930s on—deficits were run deliberately. The effects of the long decline are most noticeable during the third decade, as bottoming depressions sharply reduce revenues, in some cases beyond the ability of the government to reduce expenditures. The fourth decade reflects the upswing of prices and interest rates and, of course, the trough wars. In the fifth decade there are continued deficits as prices rise more rapidly and, of course, as the effect of the peak war is felt.

To gain a little better understanding of how the long wave influences the balance of the federal budget, we must go back through the years and examine some of the things that have happened. The most dramatic illustration of the action of the federal budget in relation to the downswing of the long wave was in the years following the Civil War. The long-wave price peak was reached in 1865, as the heavy demand for war materials began to disappear. From then on, as the downward reinforcing spiral began to take hold, the federal government began to move into the black. Prices fell, expenditures lagged behind tax collections, and surpluses mounted. Beginning in 1866 the government ran a budget surplus in every year through 1893—twenty-eight budgetary surpluses in a row! Public attitudes, of course, were one reason this was possible. It was a time of laissez faire and the unfettered dominance of American capitalism. Few disputed the idea that government should remain small and preferably weak, spending money only when necessary. The nation expanded enormously; the government did not. Another reason for the surpluses was falling prices and falling interest rates, which helped hold costs down. The Bureau of Labor Statistics Wholesale Commodity Price Index, which averaged 66.7 for the year 1866, fell to 25.4 by 1896, the year prices bottomed out. Interest rates during the thirty-year downswing phase of the long wave following the Civil War peak were cut in half, dropping from above 6 percent to about 3 percent. While some federal debt was noncallable and could only be retired by purchasing bonds in the open market, some was refunded at lower rates or retired as it came due. Interest expense, which has always been a significant factor in federal budgets, fell during all the years after the Civil War. The peak in federal interest-rate expenditures—about $140 million—came in 1867, and then declined to a low of $23 million in 1892.

As we saw earlier, long-wave downswings have been periods of protectionism and protectionism generates revenues through tariffs. In the period following the Civil War, tariffs were by far and away the largest single source of revenue. Without the income from these tariffs, it would have been more difficult to produce surpluses.

When the long waves hit bottom, the final depression of the downward phase has been so severe that federal revenues declined to the point where even drastic cuts in federal spending could not prevent a budget deficit. In the long-wave downswing following the Civil War, this deficit occurred in 1894, during the bottoming depression. In 1893 receipts were $386 million, with expenditures of $384 million. The next year expenditures were pared to $368 million, but receipts fell faster, to $306 million, producing a deficit of over $60 million, the first deficit in twenty-eight years. Similar budget deficits had been recorded at the bottom of the previous long wave. Between 1816 and 1836 there had been only three slight deficits—in 1820, 1821, and 1824. However, beginning with the Panic of 1837, when the land boom collapsed, through 1843, the year the bottoming depression ended, there was only one surplus: in 1839, the year of recovery from the collapse of 1837. As with the post–Civil War years, the severe economic reversals *forced* the government into deficits. Although every effort was made to cut expenditures, the cuts could never keep up with the drop in revenues. Excluding 1816, when military appropriations were still high, the largest federal budget during the downswing of the first wave was $31 million, in 1836. Seven years later, in 1843, at the very bottom of the long wave, federal expenditures had been slashed to $12 million, but the government still ran a deficit of over $3 million.

The pattern has been much the same in modern times. At the beginning of the last great wave, from the 1920 peak on, the usual trend of surpluses began. Prior to this there had been a string of deficits associated with World War I and with the years of upswing from the 1896 bottom. During those years there were fourteen deficits and ten surpluses, including the surplus of 1920. Every year from then through 1930 was a surplus year. The Great Depression then hit the nation so hard that although both the Hoover and, initially, the Roosevelt administrations struggled to balance the budget, deficits began to appear just as they did in the later years of previous long-wave downswings.

The government's approach to debt changed as the public reacted to the Great Depression. But it was merely a temporary switch from the usual practice of cutting back during the long-wave downswing. When the economy recovered, the man in the street wanted to see surpluses again. Had World War II not intervened, he probably would have seen a few between recessions. Once it was adjudged that the nation's economic health had been restored, the public began to regard unbalanced budgets with a wary eye. However, the upswing administrations were hard pressed to keep up with the needs, real and imagined, of the rapidly expanding economy. The two decades of upswing since 1950, particularly the 1960s, provide ample evidence that the long wave tends to be more of a factor in the balance of the federal budget than any of the usually accepted factors. It will not change. A string of surpluses following our withdrawal from Vietnam and other foreign entanglements should serve to establish this fact beyond question.

That the balance of the federal budget tends to reflect the long wave in wholesale commodity prices and interest rates may, in part, be explained logically. As the peak wars ended, a deflationary trend was set up, causing costs of government, including debt costs, to fall. Surpluses were run because taxes and tariffs were cut at the same pace at which costs fell relative to revenues. Federal budgetary surpluses would then, in turn, reinforce the downward drift. At the bottom of the long wave, depressions of such severity were experienced that federal budgets were *involuntarily* unbalanced. Coming when they did, these deficits must have helped but probably were not significant enough to cause the reversal of the deflationary trend. Once the trend of prices and interest rates began to move upward, it became a question of keeping up with the rapidly expanding needs of the economy and, to a great degree, rising public expectations.

CHAPTER 6
POLITICS
AND
PRESIDENTS

American politics have been characterized by recurring shifts between liberal and conservative dominance. The relationship between politics and the long wave is, unfortunately, inconclusive. It cannot be said that politics have so closely followed the movement of prices and interest rates that at any arbitrarily chosen point in time specific things could be expected on the political scene. It is even difficult to establish criteria for what politics are about at any point in time because the shift between dominance of liberal or conservative attitudes is usually subtle. One measure might be, for example, whether the presidency was occupied by a liberal or a conservative. Another might be the general level of interest in politics. But these are such vague indicators that any measure will, perforce, be inexact.

Nevertheless certain things have occurred in American politics that do seem to bear a relationship to the long wave. Although we cannot definitely attribute them to the long wave, they merit exploration. First, we will use as a standard of measurement the apparent liberal or conservative bent of various presidents. Obviously these are labels, even though some have been self-applied. Notwithstanding the fact that one man's liberal may be another man's conservative, there is at least fairly general agreement on which label to apply to each man who has filled the nation's highest office.

The relationship between politics and the long wave is not a continuum, but it does exist in places. Perhaps the most interesting relationship between the two has occurred at the wave peaks. This is in part, we believe, because the peak periods were times of great ferment, great issues, and great wars. If we look at the Presidents who took office on the upswing side of each long-wave peak and were still President at the time of each peak war, we find three things: all were liberals; all were important in terms of what their administrations did or how their thinking influenced future generations; all were succeeded by conservatives.

The periods and the men involved were:

MADISON Elected 1808 and 1812; liberal; succeeded by Monroe, who was elected in 1816 and was conservative.

LINCOLN Elected 1860 and 1864; liberal; succeeded by Grant, who was elected in 1868 and was conservative.

WILSON   Elected 1912 and 1916; liberal; succeeded by Harding, who was elected in 1920 and was conservative.

KENNEDY-JOHNSON† Elected 1960 and 1964; liberal; succeeded by Nixon, who was elected in 1968 and was conservative.

As we have seen earlier each long-wave peak has been followed by a decade unique in character in terms of the other decades of its wave, but rather similar to the decades in corresponding positions in other waves. The first of these periods was the period following the War of 1812, the second was the Reconstruction, and the third was the 1920s. The fourth such period has just begun; it is the 1970s. In each of the first three periods we have seen, and will see in the fourth period now beginning, a strong shift to political conservatism. Whether such attitudes form first and influence the long wave or whether the long wave influences attitudes no one can tell. But the politics and the economics of the years following the peak do resemble each other.

In 1816 the liberal period characterized by the Madison presidency ended and a conservative, James Monroe, took office. Wartime tariffs were extended, chiefly for reasons of protection, although the revenue was needed to put the budget back in balance—something both liberals and conservatives wanted.

---

†There is little doubt that John Kennedy would have been reelected and that much of his popularity spilled over onto Lyndon Johnson, who won by the largest plurality in history.

Monroe's inauguration also marked the end of Federalist rule of the country and the beginning of the reaction to federalism, a swing away from the concept of strong central government. Monroe's cabinet was, for example, composed entirely of anti-Federalists, the most famous of whom was John Quincy Adams, who served as secretary of state and became President himself in 1824.

At this first long-wave peak then, the nation apparently swung from the liberal Federalist orientation to a more conservative, states' rights approach. The primary postwar recession that began in 1819 rocked the Madison administration, but it managed to survive and win reelection in 1820, just as in later years conservatives were to experience primary postwar depression and survive.

Abraham Lincoln was, of course, a liberal and a Federalist and was President during a peak war. In the 1860s America was, as it is today, undergoing an enormous emotional catharsis, a turning point of bitter despair and frustration that had built, step-by-step, during the two decades of rising prosperity. The tension and the hate were not terminated with the war or with Lincoln's assassination, but lived on into the term of Andrew Johnson. Johnson was a Southern Democrat placed on the 1864 ticket to balance it. When Lincoln was assassinated the following April, it fell to Johnson to begin the nation's efforts to reconstruct the South.

But Johnson was plagued by radical Republicans in Congress who took a punitive approach to Southern reentry into the Union. They became irate because he favored easy reentry, as had Lincoln, and because he refused to support equal rights for the newly freed blacks. Johnson vetoed the Civil Rights Act of 1866, but this veto was overridden. From then on the radicals never let up. By mid-1868 Johnson faced impeachment on charges that were largely politically inspired. Only a margin of one vote in the Senate saved him.

The striking similarities between the assassinations of Lincoln and Kennedy and the difficulties faced by their successors, Andrew Johnson and Lyndon Johnson, go far beyond those widely discussed at the time of John Kennedy's death. Like Andrew Johnson, Lyndon Johnson started with enormous public support and gradually fell into public disfavor. There were about 100 years between the two tragedies, both of which took place just before a long-wave peak. Lincoln's death was perhaps connected more closely with the resistance to his politics than Kennedy's, although this is uncertain because the motives of Kennedy's assassin died with him. There is little doubt that Dallas was seething with hate and, while it was perhaps more extreme than other parts of the nation, it was not atypical of the conservative reaction to Kennedy's liberal ideas. Such a reaction was also the basis of Lincoln's assassination. Both were hated men, hated by conservatives for their liberal tendencies.

This hate, in both cases, was fanned by the rising tensions characteristic of periods of rising prosperity. The emotional coloration imparted to the politics of such periods is intense. As we will see later in Wilson's case, much of the emotional fury apparently unleashed at the long-wave peaks centers around the most visible symbol of politics, the Chief Executive. Lincoln and Kennedy went to premature deaths by assassins' weapons. Wilson lived on and became the unhappy recipient of the nation's scorn. That same fate was dealt to the successors of Lincoln and Kennedy.

What might have happened to Lincoln and Kennedy had they lived makes interesting speculation, given the mood of much of the nation in the years that followed, the fate of their successors (particularly Andrew Johnson), and the fate of Wilson, who died embittered and powerless. Perhaps Lincoln would have lost favor with his own party over the issue of easy reentry to the Union. Certainly this policy of Lincoln's was part of the basis for the radicals' attacks on Andrew Johnson. Perhaps John Kennedy would have been irresistibly drawn, as Lyndon Johnson was, by the promises of the generals and the rising spirit of military intervention, into the trap of an unwinnable war in Southeast Asia. Lincoln and Kennedy might have seen their popularity fade, as Wilson's did. The political polarization of the bitter liberal-conservative controversies and later the emotional letdown into spiritual exhaustion characteristic of the other side of the long-wave peak might well have engulfed both men, had not assassins' bullets claimed them first .

The election of Ulysses S. Grant in 1868 began a twenty-eight-year string of conservative Presidents— four Republicans and one Democrat—that encompassed almost the entire long-wave downswing. Indeed, it probably would have covered the whole downswing but for the fact that the incumbency of the Lincoln-Johnson administration ran into 1868. The reign of the conservatives in the White House was finally interrupted in 1896, at the wave's exact bottom, with the election of William McKinley.

Undoubtedly the worst failure the presidency has ever seen, Grant was one of the conservatives who followed the famous liberals who presided over the government at the long-wave peaks. Grant, like Harding, occupied the White House in the unique first decade of the long wave's downhill side, a period that has been marked by conservatism. Today that position is occupied by Richard Nixon.

Whether it was unconscious or whether Grant himself really understood, his administration was characterized by the most enlightened monetary and fiscal policies since the days of Alexander Hamilton. Consider the Grant administration's handling of the greenback controversy. Greenbacks were money printed during the Civil War to buy the war materials and services the federal government could not pay for through taxation and borrowing. At their peak, some $450 million worth of greenbacks were outstanding—printing-press money that played an important role in the Civil War price inflation. At the war's end there were strong feelings that the debt, including the monetary debt represented by greenbacks, should be retired as quickly as possible. Grant, however, pointed out that as the nation expanded the greenbacks would be absorbed into the normal money supply and probably go unnoticed. Considering the fact that you may have an "nth generation" greenback in your pocket at the moment, this was not a bad observation.

The years following the Civil War were characterized by monetary squabbles between the easy-money advocates, represented by farmers, small businessmen, and other members of the debtor classes, and the sound-money advocates. Grant's term extended into the depression of 1874–1879, the first post–Civil War period, during which the force of the debtor groups was felt. Grant, unlike the Harding-Coolidge administration that followed the peak of the next wave, took office three years after the Civil War peak, missed the primary postwar depression, but was on hand for the very protracted secondary one, the equivalent of the Great Depression of the 1930s.† During the depression of the 1870s there was great pressure to inflate the currency by issuing more greenbacks. It was one of the few times in American history when an economic downturn was greeted by anything but cries for a reduction in government expenditures. As might be expected it came from the agrarians, whose products, as Kondratieff pointed out, suffer the sharpest deflationary pressures in periods of long-wave downswing.

At the next long-wave peak in 1920, Woodrow Wilson was President. The last of a series of four liberals to hold office after the decisive defeat of the conservatives in 1896, Wilson moved from an aura of progres-

---

†Harding and Coolidge took office right at the 1920 peak and as a result were out of government before a *full* postwar decade had elapsed. Hoover had the misfortune of filling in the time before the secondary post-peak war depression began.

sive liberalism into the intense emotion and eventually the utter despair surrounding the peak years. Wilson, who followed Lincoln by fifty-two years and preceded John Kennedy by forty-eight, was part of the usual political syndrome involving the shift from liberalism to conservatism at the long-wave peak. While Lincoln's liberalism involved states' rights versus federalism and the issue of civil rights, Wilson, much like Kennedy, was concerned with the rights of individuals versus the giants of industrial America. Indeed Wilson's *New Freedom* was fully titled *The New Freedom from Big Business Domination* and his speeches might have, but for a few dated phrases, been those of John Kennedy five decades later.

There is no better illustration of the massive emotional shift that takes place at the long-wave peak than the one reflected in the political career of Woodrow Wilson. Elected in 1912, he was the fourth in consecutive series of liberal Presidents, and he continued the reform atmosphere that had dominated the two decades of upswing beginning with 1896. The mood of the nation favored such reforms, and Wilson successfully won congressional backing for a large reform program. When World War I broke out in Europe, no one realized what was about to happen. But the assassination of an unimportant archduke in Austria began to topple the great nations of Europe, one by one, into war. Wilson was determined to keep the United States neutral. But public opinion began to slide, first toward sympathy with the Allies, then to a demand that we join the fight. German submarine warfare nearly brought

America in. Wilson, however, managed to extract an agreement from the Germans not to continue attacks on United States shipping. In November 1916 Wilson was reelected on the slogan, "He kept us out of war." But the following year relations with Germany deteriorated, and after the announcement that they would renew their submarine attacks, efforts to maintain neutrality collapsed completely. War was declared on April 6, 1917.

Of this period Frederick Lewis Allen writes, in *The Big Change*, that "as the conflict that we now call World War I grew in fury and scope, the issues which it provoked began so to dominate the American scene that gradually the impulse toward reform was overwhelmed. Or rather, the crusading spirit was translated, by the time the United States entered the war against Germany in 1917, into making the war a crusade for freedom—or a crusade, as Woodrow Wilson put it, 'to make the World safe for democracy'.. . . The great majority of American men and women had real faith that this war could be the last one ever, that victory could bring a new day of universal freedom, and they prosecuted the war with an almost evangelical dedication."†

Initially the war was not only supported, it was idealized, and the battlegrounds of Europe became the objects of release for the tensions generated by two decades of rising prosperity. Energy previously ex-

---

†Frederick Lewis Allen, *The Big Change: America Transforms Itself, 1900–1950* (New York: First Perennial Library Edition, Harper & Row, 1969) p.93.

pended on domestic reform was channeled into a crusade, an undertaking of such high purpose that young men flocked to volunteer in huge numbers, clogging the recruiting stations and half emptying the colleges in a few days after the formal declaration by Congress.

Eventually the emotional energy that had been poured into the war was exhausted, and with the exhaustion Wilson saw his power and popularity fade. There was no exact turning point, but there were some signs that indicated the beginning of that turning, signs such as the election of a Republican-dominated House and Senate in 1918. When Wilson began to work on the peace treaty, he was at the height of his popularity. By the time it had been signed, he was in a decline from which he never recovered. The Senate, reflecting the growing appeal of isolationism, refused to ratify the treaty as it stood. The nation's concerns were clearly turning inward, away from military solutions, European entanglements, and support of an internationalist-minded Woodrow Wilson. After refusing to compromise with Henry Cabot Lodge and the rest of the Senate, Wilson made a desperate personal appeal to the nation, traveling coast to coast by rail. He collapsed during this speaking tour and was forced to cancel the balance of his trip. The public never rallied to support his position. He finished his years in the White House disillusioned and embittered.

America had not completed its emotional catharsis as 1920 opened, nor had the long wave quite reached its peak, but the peak was nearly there. The primary postwar recession, which was to bring prices and interest rates down sharply, hit in May. Frederick Lewis Allen sensed this feeling of America's pending exhaustion. "The crusading spirit was like a bank whose funds were being overdrawn," he wrote in *The Big Change.* "It lasted long enough, at the close of the war, to complete the ratification of the woman suffrage amendment and—even more remarkably—of the prize curiosity of reformist ardor, the prohibition amendment, which at the time it went into effect in January 1920, was expected by almost everybody to end once and for all the era of alcoholic drinking in America. But then, abruptly, the impulse to make over the nation and the world was discovered to have faded away. A people who had had enough of high causes and noble sacrifice to hold them for a long time decided to take things easy, to enjoy themselves; and although there remained many American idealists who would not abandon their quest, they found that they, too, were tired as well as outnumbered. The revolt of the American conscience was over."[†]

As Wilson had exemplified the progressive mood of America at the height of liberal politics and the triumph of reform, so did Sen. Warren G. Harding exemplify the new mood of America. The presidential election of 1920, which Harding won, graphically recorded the shift from one mood to the other. America was tired, war weary, and expended. The nation longed for a return to normality, or as Harding insisted on calling it, "normalcy." His vice-president, Calvin Coolidge, had

---

[†]Allen, *The Big Change,* p. 94.

attained national prominence as governor of Massachusetts by taking a hard line on the Boston police strike. Running on a "law and order" platform, the two did not just squeek into office; they won by a sizable majority over the Democratic candidates James M. Cox and Franklin D. Roosevelt. The law and order issue was strong at this point in the long wave because people were reacting to the unrest, riots, and bombings associated with the peak years.

Like Grant, who had taken charge at a similar time in the previous long wave, Harding was a conservative who took charge after the peak-war years of a liberal administration. He, too, was not very competent. But unlike the strong-willed Grant, Harding was aware of his own shortcomings and attempted to pick a cabinet of highly capable men, on whom he intended to rely. Unfortunately some of these, such as Attorney General Harry Daugherty and Interior Secretary Albert B. Fall, were not worthy of his trust. A series of scandals involving corruption of high administration officials began to break, but Harding was spared from the largest of these, the Teapot Dome Scandal, by his sudden death in August 1923. He left only one noteworthy achievement: the Washington naval disarmament conference, which established a fixed ratio of warships to be operated by major world powers. Under this significant disarmament agreement, many vessels were scrapped. A similar disenchantment with war and the military is being felt today.

Calvin Coolidge inherited the White House after Harding's death. He was, perhaps, the only man in

American politics at the time who was more suited to the job of leaving the American people alone than Warren Harding had been. Coolidge took long naps in the afternoons, almost never spoke unless forced to, and strenuously avoided making decisions. This fitted the American mood so well that Coolidge was elected President in his own right in 1924 and probably could have easily won reelection in 1928. His laissez-faire approach to business, Treasury Secretary Andrew Mellon's persistent tax cuts, and the relative prosperity characteristic of the first post-peak decade combined to impart a near-euphoric atmosphere in the 1920s. The formula was perfect.

The Harding-Coolidge era started almost exactly at the long-wave peak. Coolidge, in resisting the temptation to run for a second term of his own, unconsciously ensured his exodus from the presidency prior to the secondary post-peak depression, which began with the great stock-market crash of 1929. Grant, who in the previous wave did not take charge until 1869, some four years after the peak, was still in office for the secondary depression, which ran from 1874–1879. Grant, of course, missed the primary post-peak depression, which had fallen in on Andrew Johnson in 1865. The Harding-Coolidge administration, on the other hand, felt the full force of the first of the downswing depressions in 1920 and 1921. The situation of this administration was similar to that of the Monroe administration, which felt the primary postwar depression in 1819 but missed the more protracted secondary one, which ran from 1825 to 1829. John Quincy Adams, Monroe's conservative successor, like Herbert Hoover, Coolidge's conservative successor, had taken possession of the White House about one year before the depression occurred.

Richard Nixon took office about one year before the primary postwar recession, which has been eased by continued spending for war, space, and foreign involvement. Although this spending is gradually shrinking, the war lingers on. But there is every indication that his administration will turn out like those of his predecessors who were at the same point in the long wave.

CHAPTER 7
TURNING POINTS

Three long waves have been completed since the 1814 peak. Since that peak the trend of prices and interest rates has changed direction five times. We are now witnessing the sixth such shift. The turning points are a time of immense change, both economically and in public attitudes, in the way people think and believe. Moreover the turning points have different characteristics. Changes at the peak produce far different responses than changes at the trough. The peak is followed by a plateau decade; the trough is not, the trend simply turns and heads upward. As a result, the downswing is divided into two unequal parts and, unlike the upswing, the years at its beginning look far different economically from the years at the end.

There have been only two classic long-wave troughs —in 1844, following the first downswing, and in 1896, following the second one. They occurred fifty-two years apart. The third trough had no chance to fit the classic pattern because a major war, World War II, ended the downswing prematurely. In the first two waves, the final depression was severe. The Hungry Forties were doubtless the worst period in the fifty years between the War of 1812 and the Civil War. In 1844, however, in the depth of a depression, the economy quietly began to change direction. No great events, no speeches, no crusades heralded the change. The economy simply started to recover. Business improved, jobs opened up, prices began to rise. During the depression years the nation had been concerned with the problem of the economic system—land speculation and sound money. But then it slowly became more preoccupied with other, more political, problems—rivalry between the agrarian South and the industrial North, states' rights, free trade. The transition was remarkably easy. Just as prices and interest rates stopped going down one month and started going up the next, so did the nation, without great upheaval, switch its attention from the problems of the downswing and contraction to that of the upswing and expansion.

If the most striking thing about the shift from downtrend to uptrend is the ease with which it is accomplished, then perhaps the most significant thing about the subsequent reversal, the one at the peak, is that it is painful. This was evident not only at the Civil War peak, which followed the 1844 trough by some two decades, but it has been true in every subsequent peak reversal that followed. One has only to look at the agonies of the social and economic dislocations of the past few years to see what is in fact, an "instant replay" of what has occurred before.

There are two probable reasons why the transition is easier at the bottom than at the top. The first is that after three decades of deflation, severe depressions, and no wars, the nation is calmer. People are more concerned with the rewards of daily life. They are more thankful for things received than discontented over unfulfilled expectations. In the downswing, tomorrow may be worse; therefore today is not so bad. During the upswing, on the other hand, expectations rise faster than the economy. People become impatient with progress toward material goals and dissatisfied with those goals even before they are reached. In the upswing, tomorrow is expected to be better; today, therefore, is not acceptable.

The second reason is the location and nature of the predictable wars, which have occurred after the troughs and during or just before the peaks. As a result, trough periods, when the economy is slack, have suffered none of the economic dislocations characteristic of wartime periods, particularly periods of major wars. But during the peak the economy is overextended and tensions are high.

Nothing better illustrates the ability of a slack economy to absorb a major war than World War II. An enormous war in terms of demands on the economy, it caused relatively few dislocations. World War II put America to work again, started idle factories, and used cheap money—money the depression had driven from a lending rate of 8–10 percent down to 1 percent. World War II created a bottom and the transition from downswing to upswing was easy.

Radical politics, which have never succeeded on their own in America, have always been associated with the peak rather than the trough periods. At first glance, this might seem somewhat illogical because one tends to associate such movements with "downtrodden masses" and the suffering of a depression. But it is not the masses suffering from the effects of economic reversals who have constituted the backbone of radical politics in America. It has been an intellectual or leadership elite who, in times of prosperity, have argued that the masses were not sharing in the growing affluence. This radical leadership may or may not have come from the people, but historically its approach has generally been utopian and at times almost naïve. Utopian naïvité has held little appeal when the economy was in a slump.

Even the American Federation of Labor, which sprung up in the middle of the downswing that lasted from the Civil War nearly to the end of the nineteenth century, was largely apolitical in terms of social theory. It placed far more emphasis on that antithesis of radicalism, business unionism. The New Deal, too, despite some radical trappings, really aimed at restoring rather than destroying capitalism. FDR's reforms were the minimum judged effective, not the maximum a radical would suggest. The political activity associated with both the Vietnamese years and with the World War I peak, on the other hand, more nearly typifies the kind of activity one would call radical politics. Such movements have failed in the past and are failing now chiefly because they always fall on unfertile ground. As long as the bright promise of escape from poverty is held open to those capable of escaping, revolution will be a slow seller. In America what might have become an angry, capable leadership of the poor has always been vented off by the opportunities that the society held out to the few who were strong enough, intelligent enough, and if necessary ruthless enough to seize them. The radical leaders who have historically been left behind in America have been so far too inept, too idealistic, too utopian in their orientation to succeed in the hard business of convincing other men that their lot is bad enough to risk death in an effort to change it.

The case of the blacks in America during the upswing years is a good example of what has happened with minorities and the poor in general. When pressure built up that could have led to revolution, the nation's leadership responded by opening opportunities for talented blacks, diverting the best talent into the establishment and away from violent revolution.

Politics at the troughs have been tame in comparison to the peaks. Upheavals during downswing periods have not been specifically associated with the *end* of the downswing. Prosperity breeds tension, discontent, and the revolutionary spirit, but deflation seems to breed the opposite—a much calmer public, a more resolute approach to life, and an endorsement of established institutions and values.

Prices and interest rates change more spectacularly around the peaks than around the troughs. It is not hard to see that the effect on prices and interest rates has been pronounced, for each peak has been associated with a long, bitterly fought war and followed by a recession. Wholesale prices, using an index in which 1957–1959 prices equal 100, behaved this way:

	Year	Index
	1809	45.4
FIRST PEAK	1814	62.3
	1819	47.7

The next two peaks showed the same general configuration:

	Year	Index
	1859	34.3
SECOND PEAK	1864	74.7
	1869	56.9

	Year	Index
	1915	38.0
THIRD PEAK	1920	84.5
	1925	56.6

Prices at the troughs do show considerable deterioration, but the extent of deflation does not approach the extent of inflation at the peaks. Prices are unable to go down as rapidly in the midst of a market glut, which is what occurs in a depression, as they can rise during the scramble that occurs during the superheated prosperity of war. The trough figures are as follows:

	Year	Index
	1838	37.2
FIRST TROUGH	1843	25.4
	1848	26.5
	1891	30.6
SECOND TROUGH	1896	25.4
	1901	30.2

The third trough was, of course, obliterated by the oncoming demand of the pre-World War II rush to arms. For the year 1939 the index stood at 42.2, about half of the 84.5 of the peak year, 1920. It appears that, at this point, prices were at about the same relative level as they were in the two previous waves. Going back fifty-two years (one wave) from 1939 to 1887, we find that the index stood at 31.2, down from 74.7 at the Civil War peak. Moving back 104 years (two waves), we find that the wholesale price level stood at 36.9 in 1835, down from the 1814 peak of 62.3. In short, before World War II, prices seemed to be heading toward a similar bottoming process during the 1940s.

The economy probably reacts with more distinct price changes at the peak than at the trough for two reasons. First is the nature of prices. There is no ceiling on how far prices can rise; in the face of demand that cannot be filled because the economy is operating at full capacity, it is easy to increase prices because each increase usually means more profit. On the other hand prices can be cut only so far (to zero), and price cuts cost money. In a deflationary period, even if rapid price cuts could be made without incurring financial ruin, the resultant demand for goods would not increase rapidly enough to make it worthwhile.

Second is the nature of inflation and deflation. The economy is ill prepared to deal with inflation created by more demand for goods and services. Overextended, the economy has little resistance to inflationary pressure. Money is scarce, employment is high, industrial capacity is fully used. To top it off the government, fighting a wave peak-war, bids against the public for goods and services, thus adding to the inflation. At the trough, however, the economy is overcontracted, like a compressed spring, and like a spring it can be pushed down only so far.

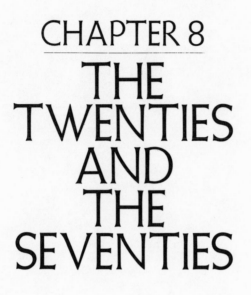

CHAPTER 8

THE TWENTIES AND THE SEVENTIES

America—its economy, its tensions, its mood—is at the same relative position in the long wave as it was at the end of World War I, the Civil War, and the War of 1812. The closest parallels, however, can be drawn with the period of the World War I peak: only then was the United States predominantly industrial, predominantly dependent on a money economy, as it is now.

The one and perhaps the only substantial difference between the World War I period and the present is that the first war came to an emphatic end (in November 1918) but the Vietnam War, although psychologically over, lingers on. In the long run, however, the outcome will be the same. Americans will be utterly disillusioned by war and will not easily be led into another crusade "to make the world safe for democracy," "to stop the spread of communism," or to do whatever another call to arms might demand. The protracted Vietnam War has also generated an unusual reaction in the economy. As happened during World War I, the wartime demand has taxed the economy beyond its ability to produce and has created a demand-pull inflation. In response to this inflation, labor extracted stiff wage increases. Next, as war demand eased, both during the post–World War I period and the present, the economy moved into the primary postwar downturn of the long wave. The situation of the early 1970s is not, however, really postwar; it is deescalation. There is no longer excessive wartime demand, but the economy does not completely lack the stimulation of some military expenditure. The result has been a sluggish economy that reflects slackening demand combined with nagging inflation problems. Such residual inflationary pressure would be quickly killed by a sharp downturn, but it has survived this mild one.

Yet the conduct and the temperament of the society is already much the same as it was in the years right after World War I. Malcolm Cowley, in *Exiles Return,* notes that the literary bohemians who lived and worked in New York's Greenwich Village prior to World War I had a philosophy that virtually comprised an entire system of ideas, a doctrine that after the war became a model for much of the rest of America. Today nearly the same system of ideas has sprung up again, flourishing in the climate provided by the two decades of nearly continuous prosperity in the 1950s and 1960s. The ideas of the adventuresome and less inhibited will once again become the cornerstone concepts of the 1970s. Today's terminology is slightly changed from the last long-wave peak, but the ideas are so similar that one has little difficulty recognizing them. As Cowley put it, "Greenwich Village was not only a place, mood, a way of life; like all Bohemias, it was also a doctrine. . . . By 1920, it had become a system of ideas that could be roughly summarized as follows:

"1. *The Idea of Salvation by the Child.* Each of us at birth has special potentials which are slowly crushed and destroyed by a standardized society and mechanical methods of teaching. If a new educational system can be introduced, one by which children are encouraged to develop their own personalities, to blossom freely like flowers, then the world will be saved by this new, free generation.

"2. *The Idea of Self-Expression.* Each man's, each woman's purpose in life is to express himself, to realize his full individuality through creative work and beautiful living in beautiful surroundings.

"3. *The Idea of Paganism.* The body is a temple in which there is nothing unclean, a shrine to be adorned for the ritual of life.

"4. *The Idea of Living for the Moment.* It is stupid to pile up treasures that we can enjoy only in old age, when we have lost the capacity for enjoyment. Better to seize the moment as it comes, to dwell in it intensely, even at the cost of future suffering.

"5. *The Idea of Liberty.* Every law, convention or rule of art that prevents self-expression or the full enjoyment of the moment should be shattered and abolished. Puritanism is the great enemy. The crusade against puritanism is the only crusade with which free individuals are justified in allying themselves.

"6. *The Idea of Female Equality.* Women should be the economic and moral equals of men. They should have the same pay, the same working conditions, the same opportunity for drinking, smoking, taking or dismissing lovers.

"7. *The Idea of Psychological Adjustment.* We are unhappy because we are maladjusted, and maladjusted because we are repressed. If our individual repressions can be removed—by confessing them to a Freudian psychologist—then we can adjust ourselves to any situation, and be happy in it.

"8. *The Idea of Changing Place.* 'They do things better in Europe.' England and Germany have the wisdom of old cultures; the Latin peoples have admirably preserved their heritage."†

Today many people—young and old—have embraced most of these ideas, which form the credo of the "Now Generation." One needs only to compare Charles A. Reich's *The Greening of America* with Malcolm Cowley's work to see the parallels. Reich, of

---

†Malcolm Cowley, *Exiles Return* (New York: Viking Press, 1951), pp. 59–61.

THE TWENTIES AND THE SEVENTIES

course, focuses on the "revolutionized" youth of America. He correctly sees them as the forerunners of society, the heralds of a system of values that, like the values of Cowley's pre–World War I Greenwich Village, will in the decade following the war become the basis for a new value system that will be adopted by most Americans. The adoption, however, will be of a modified version of youth's values—not the total acceptance Reich predicts. Nevertheless it will set the mood, the outlook, the psychological climate for the 1970s and will eventually change both the politics and the economics of America.

To see the parallels, however, we should examine Cowley's points and compare them with the psychology, attitudes, and issues of today's forerunners of society.

The Idea of Salvation by the Child. Cowley said that the system of ideas embraced by the Greenwich Village bohemians implied that "each of us at birth has special potentials which are slowly crushed and destroyed by a standardized society and mechanical methods of teaching." Says Reich on the dehumanization of man: "If anyone doubts these words, let him look at the faces of America. Stand at a commuter train station and see the blank, hollow, bitter faces. Sit in a Government cafeteria and see the faces set in rigidity, in unawareness, in timid compliance, or bureaucratic obstinacy; the career women with all their beauty fled, the men with all their manhood drained. We do not look at faces very often in America, even less than we look at ruined rivers and devastated hills."† On teaching methods: "School is intensely concerned with training students to stop thinking and start obeying. Any course that starts with a textbook and a teacher and ends with an examination runs this danger unless pains are taken to show students that they are supposed to think for themselves; in most school and college classes, on the other hand, thinking for oneself is actually penalized, and the student learns the value of repeating what he is told. Public school is 'obedience school'; the student is taught to accept authority without question. . . ."‡

The idea of salvation by the child is perhaps the strongest of the recurring themes. The popularization of the notion that the child possesses special qualities that adults do not gives birth to a youth cult. The youth cult in America today is, as it was before, the product of prosperity and it has much in common with the one of Cowley's day. One similarity is ignorance of the origins of the problems of society. During the period of prosperity of the long-wave upswing, society is subject to a vast amount of disorientation caused by an accelerating rate of change. This is disquieting to everyone, young and old. The older, more conservative, elements of society tend to resist such change, while younger people tend to encourage it. Moreover, problems that perhaps had originated, at least in part, in events, customs and values thousands of years old become, in the eyes of the young, the direct responsibility

---

†Charles A. Reich, *The Greening of America* (New York: Random House, 1970), p. 151–152.
‡Reich, p. 131.

of their parent's generation. This is ironic not only because their parent's generation is no more responsible for the problems than they are, but because the clamor for more change is heard only after changes have begun to occur, not before.

Another similarity between today's youth cult and that of the 1920s is the notion of comradeship among the young, the idea that the young are somehow special and endowed with wisdom solely by virtue of being young. This wisdom is thought somehow to have been denied to older generations, to parents and grandparents, and is therefore unexplainable. It is the combination of the notion that there is something unique in being young and the ignorance of the past that has created today's youth cult, just as it created the one in the 1920s. Slogans such as "don't trust anyone over thirty" embody the idea that the young are a group apart having knowledge, rights, and privileges that those older than they, by virtue of the fact that they are older, cannot understand.

The youth cult of the last long-wave peak started as a crusade but ended as a party. The romantic ideas that led many young people to volunteer for military service were soon dealt a severe blow when they learned what wars were really about. This disillusionment with war grew stronger in the 1920s and the war was increasingly criticized. Books such as *All Quiet on the Western Front* and *Paths of Glory* showed war's brutal, dehumanizing effect upon men who struggled to survive in the mud and fear of the trenches. Forgotten was the idealism of 1917, an idealism that smacked of the pre–Civil War

South and its refusal to face the fact that cavalry charges alone could not defeat the industrial machine of the North. The Vietnam War, which had some supporters among the young at first, has evoked the same type of reaction that World War I evoked after 1918— a sense of being fed up with foreign entanglements. This feeling was a major reason for the incredibly rapid decline in Woodrow Wilson's popularity. The time had simply arrived when the public, led by youth, had tired of war. It is so again today.

After World War I there was a rebirth of good times, a putting aside of the cares of war and struggle for what turned into a seemingly endless party. The earlier crusade "to make the world safe for democracy" turned into the era of the flapper, the hip flask, and jazz. The pressures of the upswing had eased—inflation was over, the "great Red scare" was over, politics were quickly forgotten—and still there was prosperity. It was in this atmosphere that the young and the not-so-young who followed their pace moved from the concerns of the hectic peak years and began to have fun. It will be so again in the 1970s.

The Idea of Self-Expression. This concept, now sometimes called "do your own thing," is another that took firm root in the prosperous years of both long-wave upswings. During periods of depression, dreadful economic insecurity renders almost meaningless the idea of self-expression and the idea that a man's life-work should be important.

The ideal of self-expression, however, flourishes

when times are good, and it means far more than merely expression in the arts. The idea of pursuing an occupation or a way of life that leads to creative self-fulfillment, freed from the restrictions of past attitudes, is an infectious one in times of plenty. The old roads to old careers seem increasingly dull and unrewarding. Moreover, with the rise of the long wave concerns about security are swept away. There is decreasing concern over basic material subsistence because everyone believes he can get a job. Under such conditions people become more preoccupied with themselves and with a search for meaning in their life. It soon becomes evident to many, particularly the young who have experienced nothing but prosperity, that most work involves little direct contribution to one's fellow man, little self-expression, and little originality.

The results of this revelation take several forms. One reaction is to shift from work as the center of preoccupation and to reach toward leisure-time activities. These, of course, require the expenditure of both time and money, something the years of prosperity give to nearly every worker. Travel, boating, camping, hobbies, and spectator sports become the self-expression of the fully employed, well-paid American who is bored with his job and no longer concerned about losing it. Self-expression for the more sophisticated, better educated, may in part be fulfilled in work or may be vented in more complex pursuits.

For still others, the move toward self-expression may entail changing professions, such as a move to teaching; or it may, particularly for the younger members of the working group, emerge as a whole new life, such as moving to Vermont or the Rockies to farm. Whatever form the movement toward self-expression may take, it is evident that for most it would be totally impossible, probably even beyond contemplation, if the long wave were in a downswing posture rather than one of high prosperity.

In *The Greening of America* Reich laments the lack of self-expression in America today. "The real tragedy of the lost self in America" he writes, "is not that of the professional middle class, who have had all the advantages, but the tragedy of the white-collar and blue-collar worker, who never had any chance. . . . Imprisoned in masks, they endure unutterable loneliness. Their lives are stories of disappointed hopes, hopes disintegrating into the bitterness and envy that is ever-present in even the most casual conversation of the worker. If they had an individual excellence or greatness, in some area, it has been passed over by society. They are Joan Baez or Bob Dylan, working in a bank or a filling station until their minds and bodies have forgotten the poetry that once was in them."†

Moreover, Reich says, this denial of self-expression is produced by the whole educational-career process. "Training toward alienation, from elementary school onward," he writes, "reaches its climax when the student is forced to make his choice, first of a college major, then of a career. Surrounding these moments is a gradually built-up picture of man as a creature who

---

†Reich, *The Greening of America*, p. 151.

has a single 'right' vocation in life, the vocation for which he is 'best fitted,' and for which he can be aptitude-tested and trained. The choice is surrounded by great anxiety and doubt, particularly because the student may find that his own nature fails to conform to the expected norm."†

The Idea of Paganism. The idea of paganism is not as significant now as it was at the time of the 1920 long-wave peak or in the decade that followed, a decade that saw such rear-guard attempts at enforcing Christian doctrine as the Scopes trial in Tennessee. Today established Christianity no longer represents a major force to be contended with and, aside from some customs, has largely been ignored in the frenzy of social upheaval, self-examination, and radical solutions.

Today's young people have not opposed Christianity, they have simply turned away from it and have replaced it with mysticism and adherence to various forms of Oriental religions. Today it is common in nearly every large American city to see small bands of young men and women, wearing pale orange-colored robes, begging on street corners while they chant the "Hari Krishna."

The occult, too, has drawn followers in these years of prosperity. Black magic, witchcraft, devil worship, astrology, and the tarot have all crept into ordinary conversations and, in a harmless way, into most ordinary lives.

Equally important is the search for more personal

---

†Reich, *The Greening of America*, p. 138–139.

forms of religious experience, either through medita-
tion, psychedelic drugs, or techniques of sensory over-
load and sensory deprivation. Virtually all of this
is taking place outside of the Christian churches and
other religious institutions. It is not quite the "paganism" of Cowley's 1920s, but it is far from the
traditional, institutionalized religion of modern Christianity.

The Idea of Living for the Moment. Young people
have always lived for the moment; part of growing up
is accepting the idea that one must face the future. To
a great degree the psychological willingness to grow up
appears to depend on the condition of the economy. In
times of plenty the tendency is to prolong one's youth,
which might better be called preadulthood. It is not
hard to see why. Despite the frustrations and dislocations of the peak-war years and the years immediately
after the peak, prosperity is pleasant. There is plenty:
plenty of money, plenty to eat, plenty of places to go.

Strongly interwoven with the youth cult is the notion
that the quest for security and the accumulation of
wealth is the business of the old. Armed with an ignorance that only the arrogance of the young can support,
it has been the temptation of every generation to look
at their seniors and choose not to be like them. It falls
uniquely to the children of prosperity, however, to shun
the accumulation of wealth, for only they have never
felt the intense pangs of being forced to do without.
"Only those who don't have to worry about it think that
money is unimportant," Dr. Bruno Bettelheim of the

University of Chicago said in *Vogue* magazine (August 1, 1970); "one can't be said to have *no* money if one knows one can get it if necessary. One can easily despise money, if others pay for the needed services."

When the idea of living for the moment overtakes the popular mind in the 1970s, as it is beginning to, the nation's heroes will be those who can bridge the gap between the carefree young, who can afford to live for the moment because there is little else they must do, and the rest of the population, who would only too eagerly unburden themselves of their responsibilities. Joe Namath, star quarterback for the New York Jets, is one such transitional hero. "Joe is not only in tune with the rebellious attitude of the young, he doubles it," wrote James Reston in *The New York Times*. "He defies both the people who hate playboys and the people who hate bullyboys. He is something special: a long-haired hard hat, the antihero of the sports world . . . he defies all the old-fashioned rules. . . . He was not like the old moral sports heroes—the Reverend Bob Richards arguing on television that sports, religion, and the breakfast food for champions were all the same thing. He was not even like Babe Ruth or Walter Hagen, who tried to conceal their alcoholic adventures. He ran his bars and his football on the same track and at the same time, defying all the old assumptions and moralities. . . . He is a significant symbol because he is following the contemporary notion that anything that succeeds is right."

And that, precisely, is what the idea of living for the moment will be about in the 1970s: defying all the old assumptions and moralities because they no longer seem relevant. The old rules were built to guard against and guide one through hard times. In good times they look ridiculous and indeed, if good times were to continue indefinitely, the old rules would have little function.

The Idea of Liberty. Now more commonly called freedom, the idea of liberty has had a strong impact on the young. As they grow up and as their ideas spread through proselytizing, all America will feel the impact. This has already begun, but by the time popularization is complete, freedom will move more from the present antiestablishment sentiment to a broader, less political interpretation. Because the man in the street is becoming more aware of the concept of the establishment, the industrial state, and the military complex, the concept of freedom from the influence of giant institutional forces will have great appeal. A reordering of national priorities will partly result from the acceptance by the man in the street of the idea of freedom, freedom from the influence of the military, industrial, and political forces that seemed to get out of control from the middle 1960s on. It will be with the backing of the man in the street that funds for and laws against pollution are passed, glamour projects such as moon landings take a back seat to an expansion of mass transit, and inflation is brought under control. In these ways the world of the early revolutionary will be adopted by virtually everyone.

In the 1920s the idea of liberty was concerned largely with the laws and mores associated with puritanism and its later-day incarnation, Victorianism. When throwing out the old and bringing in the new, such ideas of the past were important targets. People had not yet experienced the ill effects of modern times, at least to the degree that "progress" might actually be identified as the villain. That distinction history reserved for future rebels; the young of the 1920s concentrated on moving society into modern times. To do this it was necessary to move against the agents of the past, against the puritanical restrictions on the freedoms of thought, of sex, of movement, of dress. Puritanism-Victorianism was a code challenged by a new system, and, like any rebels, the challengers raised the cry of freedom.

The significant differences between the idea of liberty in vogue fifty years ago and the idea of freedom today lie only in the nature of what the rebels rebel against. In both cases prosperity provided the vehicle. The intervening years saw the New Deal attack the values of the establishment in a way the rebels of the twenties never had, and the New Deal attack formed the ideological underpinnings for the attack of the sixties and seventies.

The twenties' rebellion had been against moral, ethical, religious restrictions. The New Deal attacked something entirely different: privilege. It sought not to form a truly new order but to reform an old one that had apparently become inoperative. The New Deal sought to redistribute wealth, not to champion the cause of the disadvantaged but to get the existing system working again. It saw the rich as the cause of the Great Depression because they held onto their money, and because they did not spend, the economy began to underconsume. To get it started again, the theory was, tax wealth away from the rich and spend. Far less concern was expressed for the poor than for members of the working class who were unemployed.

Ignorant of the long wave in economics, the New Deal was as wrong about the basic causes of the Great Depression as it was about the villains. The real impact of the depression and the New Deal philosophy did not, however, take place during the depression. FDR's economic measures did not cure the depression; time and Adolf Hitler did that. The New Deal did, however, make targets of wealth and privilege. It laid the groundwork for the broad development of an American social conscience.

It was not until the full rush of prosperity began to hit in the late 1950s that this consciousness began to develop as a national philosophy. As prosperity made the gap between rich and poor more apparent, the plight of the poor, the disadvantaged, and the disenfranchised became more than could be tolerated in silence. The most conspicuous poor, of course, were the blacks. They were the first to cry for freedom, and it was their predicament that dramatically inspired the revolutionary consciousness of the sixties: if such poverty and lack of opportunity could exist in times of rising prosperity, if so little progress was being made by the blacks when so much progress was being made by others, then perhaps something was wrong with the system. The idea quickly captured the attention and the energies of the young. Out of the awareness of black repression grew an awareness of repression of other groups. Then, as prosperity rose tensions rose, and spread to other areas. The Vietnam War expanded and domestic war resistance was born, grew, and strengthened. Students saw colleges as giant "education factories" unconcerned with human values. Women began to demand equality.

The Idea of Female Equality. Now called women's liberation, the idea of female equality has paralleled the black struggle for equality and, like other revolutions, has derived its impetus from prosperity. In the earlier struggle for women's equality, the depression that began in 1929 simply dissolved the issue. It did not reappear again until the early 1960s, when Betty Friedan exhumed it in *The Feminine Mystique.* It was not by accident, however, that the fiftieth anniversary of the certification of the Nineteenth Amendment, which gave women the right to vote, took place in the midst of furor over the current women's lib movement. It was at the peak of the last wave that the first-round victory (the Nineteenth Amendment) was won, and it is at this present long-wave peak that the push for women's equality is moving again.

In his proclamation of August 26, 1970, marking the victory of women's suffrage, President Nixon noted, "it is hard for any of us living in 1970 to imagine a time when women did not vote. Yet for more than seventy-five years, American women faced adversity, ridicule, and derision on every level of our society as they sought this precious right." But what seemed obvious in 1970 did not seem so in 1920. Today's women argue that the issues of equal wages, abortion on demand, day care centers, and equal job opportunity are obvious needs too and that they are being systematically deprived of these things by a society that treats them unequally.

There are signposts of progress that, while they are not necessarily a source of much satisfaction to the woman who feels she is the victim of sex discrimination, do nevertheless indicate we have come a long way from the time of Susan B. Anthony. Looking back to those days of the beginning of the female equality movement, we find that it began to build strength in the years of prosperity prior to the Civil War peak. Miss Anthony personally began her attacks on the exclusion of women from the voting booths in the late 1830s, when she was seventeen years old. But the movement did not gain popular support until the 1850s when, denied membership in the Sons of Temperance, Miss Anthony organized the Daughters of Temperance. During the Civil War Miss Anthony, the daughter of a Quaker abolitionist, formed the Women's Loyal League, which was strongly abolitionist as well as feminist. In the years following the Civil War peak, as the long wave moved into its downswing phase, Miss Anthony traveled and lectured extensively; but she was never able to excite the imagination of the public enough to rally the necessary votes in behalf of female equality.

It was not until the economy moved into the upswing again in the two decades prior to the World War I wave peak that the idea of female equality again began to catch on. The voting issue was of course the most obvious, and after the war there was little chance that significant opposition could be gathered to suppress it. But votes for women were only the tip of the iceberg. When the revolt against the old order got under way after the war, female equality began to come into its own.

"It was the girls who spearheaded it," Frederick Lewis Allen wrote in *The Big Change*. "Did mothers think of corsets as the armour of respectability? A great many daughters decided that dancing without a corset was much more personal and satisfactory. Did mothers think young girls should not drink? Daughters found that a gulp of illegal whiskey from the hip flask of a swain in a parked sedan added an excellent note of zest to the proceedings. Did mothers converse in ladylike circumlocutions? Daughters talked right out about sex and the libido, the latter being a word one got from Freud, who had said, according to report, that repressions were bad for you. Had mothers been brought up in the era of long skirts, when the exposure of an ankle to the public gaze had been regarded as a virtual invitation to masculine lust? Daughters reveled in the emancipation of the new style, which by the middle of the 1920s had lifted the hemline all the way to the knee.

"In a few short years American women in general changed almost unrecognizably in appearance. As late as 1919 they had worn amply cut, ankle-length dresses over such underpinnings as corset covers, envelope chemises, and petticoats; they had worn their hair long, and had needed hatpins; and their daytime stockings had been mostly made of black (or brown, or green, or blue) cotton or lisle; silk stockings were considered somewhat luxurious. By the latter 1920's young women had reduced the yardage of their garments by one-half, were increasingly wearing silk or rayon underwear, and sought desperately to look pencil slim. They wore their hair short-bobbed or boyishly shingled—and made frequent visits to that rising institution, the beauty parlor, which had come into its own following the widespread acceptance of the permanent wave. And since the early Twenties they had been unanimously addicted to what proved to be the most durable fashion innovation of our times—flesh-colored stockings. (From their color came the term 'cheesecake' for leggy photography.) Older women followed these changes more slowly, and in some cases with a reluctant feeling that they were succumbing to a pernicious cult of youth. But there was no resisting the trend."†

The 1920s also freed women to work even if they did not have to. It freed women to smoke if they cared to, to drink, to speak, and to have fun in a way that had previously been the exclusive province of the male. Most of these things were never the public issue that voting rights was. Women simply began to do them. They were considered chic. Although the women's equality movement fizzled in the downswing of the 1930s, lasting and substantial freedoms had been won so that when the upswing returned, there was not as far to go. As Frederick Lewis Allen noted in the early 1950s, "by present day standards the social conduct of those days was not particularly loose; much more astonishing to us, in retrospect, is the code of Puritanical restraint against which

---

†Allen, *The Big Change*, p. 119–120.

the youngsters of the 1920s were rebelling. Which is another way of saying that, although there have been considerable changes in the accepted modes of social conduct since the 1920s, it was during that decade that something approaching the present code was established. Yet the atmosphere was different then; there was an air of novelty and self-conscious experiment about the relaxing of the code which was intensely exciting to the participants and shocking to observers who were out of step with the change."†

Women's lib today is more concerned with the right to live and work as an equal in a man's world than its predecessor was fifty years ago. Today, building on the base of the 1920s, which had in turn been built on the base of the 1850s, 1860s, and 1870s, the issues comprise an attack on the real resistance to female equality. The arguments about voting, drinking, smoking, and sex were concerned only with personal freedoms. The arguments of today concerning equal job opportunities and pay, the right to decide on giving birth to a child or not, and a place to care for a child while its mother works are what is at issue in the equality question. The women's equality movement of the twenties may have won the right for women to do what they wanted to, but the women's lib movement of today seeks to give them the wherewithal to do it.

The Idea of Psychological Adjustment. The idea of psychological adjustment is not as startling today as it was in the twenties because it is an accepted fact.

---

†Allen, *The Big Change*, p. 120.

As in Cowley's day, the belief still holds that maladjustment is the result of repression. No one has argued this point more emphatically than Charles Reich, who believes that the corporate state is guilty of repressions on a mass scale and that such repressions are the cause of much socially maladjusted conduct, crime in particular. Whereas the 1920s were heavily influenced by Freudian concepts, today's climate tends to be more socio-politico-economic in its orientation. The thesis of *The Greening of America* is, more than anything else, one of psychological adjustment, adjustment to a new state of mind that Reich dubs Consciousness III. His chief villain, the corporate state, is repressing the people; release from this repression, says Reich, requires a change of consciousness, a new view of man.

This change is already occurring. The intense growth of the past two decades, its prosperity and its precipitation of change, have brought the basic values of latter-day capitalism into question. Yet, because the old order has been found wanting and a new rationale has not been created to support the new capitalism, many people are confused. There has been created what Daniel Bell of Harvard University has called "the cultural contradiction." "The ultimate support for any social system is the acceptance of a moral justification of authority," Bell writes. "The older justifications of a bourgeois society lay in the defense of private property. But the 'New Capitalism' of the twentieth century has lacked such moral grounding."

It is, of course, lack of such moral justification that

the younger generation are attacking when they attack the establishment.

The Idea of Changing Place. The idea of changing place, of mobility, has taken two forms. The first is the same as was seen in the 1920s—an exodus to foreign countries—and the reasons for it are similar. One reason is exposure. World War I exposed many a farm boy to the delights and sophistications of France, which generated the desire to return. Although today's peak war is taking place in an area that few will ever wish to return to, exposure to other countries, to the delights of difference, elegance, beauty, and surprise is available through commercial jet travel. The "youth fare" will move anyone from the East Coast of the United States to Europe and back for less than $200. Once there, it is almost *de rigueur* to bicycle, backpack, hitch, or bum one's way around. The past exclusivity of grand tours for the wealthy few—the first-class restaurants with three stars from *Guide Michelin*, the Ritz, and six pieces of luggage—meant that few could go and very few would return to stay. Today's low air fare, the rucksack, and the youth hostel mean that tens of thousands will eventually go, and some will surely want to stay.

The other reason is the tension of living in the United States. "Pushed by the problems of day-to-day living here and pulled by the promise of a more satisfying way of life abroad, many of New York's most capable citizens are giving up their jobs, careers, homes and friends to resettle overseas," *The New York Times* reported late in 1970. "This new generation of expatriots is young, middle-class, well-educated, energetic and—perhaps most important for their decision to leave New York—committed to forms of self-realization they find either difficult or impossible to achieve here."

The second form that the idea of changing place has taken is the movement from middle-class suburbia to a "new life" in the open land or in more exotic surroundings. Illustrations of this are urban and rural communes and the whole back-to-the-land movement. The idea of the simple, clean life has enormous appeal. How wonderful to smell wood smoke early on a chilly morning, to hear only the distant bark of a dog at night. But these things do not really constitute farming and ranching. Farming can be tough, discouraging, and almost dehumanizing work. Farmers live less with nature than on it and frequently treat the earth as an adversary rather than a friend. For the city dweller desiring a change of place, visions of bucolic harmony are often quickly smashed by the reality of rural life, where the manure pile is apt to enjoy the vista while the farmhouse overlooks a drab spot in the hollow.

As a result of these hidden realities, most urban Americans who will try the rural life are likely to return quickly. The sojourns, however, are the embodiment of the idea of changing place, an idea symptomatic of the times that surround and follow a long-wave peak. At such times the changes created by two decades of prosperity raise important questions about one's values and the conduct of one's life. The place in which one lives is a part of this, and the movement from urban to rural places is a symbolic, as well as real, rejection of the products and results of the changes of the long-wave upswing. Whether to Europe or to the farm, the idea of changing place is an effort to escape from the way things are or, more exactly, from the way things have become. It is a by-product of prosperity that few would have envisioned three decades ago, but the momentous prosperity of the long-wave upswing made it an inevitability, just as much of what will happen during the next ten years is virtually inevitable.

CHAPTER 9
SHATTERING SOME MYTHS

Recognizing that the long wave exists will require new attitudes and new approaches to a variety of problems. Inflation, for example, has always been one of the great menaces to a stable society. Most people are afraid of inflation because they do not know what causes it and they exaggerate what it can do.

Those who fear inflation invariably cite the great post–World War I inflation in Germany as the classic example of what can happen to a nation when inflation gets out of hand. But no one knows exactly when inflation is in fact out of hand, much less how it gets there. South American countries, where the value of the currency has been deteriorating at several times the rate that ours has, have yet to disintegrate economically. The idea that inflation is all bad is shaky at best. Only those living on fixed incomes suffer. Those earning money generally make out better than they would if prices remained stable because, while prices do rise, wages rise more, even after taxes. Take the example of a newspaper reporter whose wages are covered by the American Newspaper Guild. If he had started to work in 1948, his beginning wage on a large metropolitan daily would have been, as fixed by the guild contract, $50 a week. If he remained as a reporter, never receiving a merit increase or a promotion, in 1971 he would be earning $325.83 a week under the guild contract.

Similarly, the average weekly pay of manufacturing production workers in this country has gone up from $53.88 in 1949 to $133.73 in 1970, or 148 percent. The Consumer Price Index in the same period, however, went up from 71.4 to 116.3, or 63 percent. So even after higher prices, the workingman has been way ahead.

Inflation also seems to improve the material quality of life. Switzerland, for example, is one of the few nations to experience virtually no inflation during the period of the upswing in the years since World War II. At first glance no inflation might seem an ideal situation, but this price and interest stability has been at the expense of little improvement in the material quality of Swiss life. Today, as many Americans reexamine material goals, economic growth, and quantity of output in light of such social costs as pollution, no growth may appear highly desirable. Most Americans, however, want an improved material standard of living and would have resisted any measures which would halt the upswing of the long-wave price trend.

If price stabilization had been distasteful during the normal period of the upswing, the American people would find deflation even less pleasant. In earlier chapters we discussed the past effects of long-wave downswings (the kind of period we are now entering), when prices fell rather than rose. After a long period of inflation a decline in prices may sound appealing, but history shows that that appeal is based on misconceptions. Although capitalism is changing, large business enterprises are still managed by professionals who run corporations owned by other peoples with funds generated in part by profits and in part by borrowing. Rising prices favor both profit and borrowed money. To take a simple example, let us say it costs you, a manufacturer, $10 to make one widget. If competition forces you to sell it for $10 you will show no profit. But if, while you are making that widget, inflation jacks the price to $10.50, your costs may go up but you will probably still be able to make a profit and *for no reason other than rising prices.* Conversely, when prices fall, it is not only harder to show a profit because prices do not bail you out, it is hard to keep from showing losses on operations that might otherwise break even. Borrowed money has the same effect. If prices rise after you borrow money, you benefit because you have invested in equipment that stabilizes some of your production costs while the selling costs of the goods produced rises. But in a deflationary period this leverage works just as hard against you. What you make must sell for less, but your production costs—which include interest on money borrowed for equipment—are fixed at the higher level of the inflationary period.

In general the effects of inflation are not so destructive as most people believe them to be. Inflation is more a problem at the very end of the long wave than it is at the beginning. The final burst that results when a fully extended domestic economy is forced to fight a war causes prices and interest rates to spurt, and these spurts in turn put pressure on wage earners, who demand large increases. The overall effect is both frightening and confusing because of the public's basic misunderstanding about the real nature of inflation. To many, the sight of workers pushing for huge increases is alarming because they believe that these increases will cause more price increases, which will begin a chain reaction ending only in runaway inflation. But looking at inflation in terms of the long wave, we see this cannot now happen. In addition to the leveling of the long-wave upswing in prices soon to occur, the real causes of the inflation—the huge military and space expenditures during the already high prosperity of the late 1960s—will not be duplicated. Without these there are more than adequate production facilities to meet the demands of the private and nonmilitary public sectors.

Contrary to public fears prices do not rise because of

past price increases. Inflation does not feed upon itself. Prices rise because of shortages of labor, industrial capacity, and raw materials. When the private sector of the economy is fully utilizing the supply of labor, industrial capacity, and raw materials, *and* at the same time the government begins to fight a war, prices, responding to the law of supply and demand, must rise. But when the military demands are withdrawn or reduced to a tiny fraction of their former size (as will be the case in the 1970s), surpluses of production facilities, raw materials, and labor will develop. Rapidly rising prices and a sizable industrial overcapacity cannot coexist for a protracted period of time.

As the Vietnam War winds down, however, we have what might seem to be such coexistence—rising prices and a recession, which of course is the name applied to a nationwide surplus of industrial output and labor. But a closer look reveals that what is actually happening is that the military-space industries and those closely related to them are hard hit because they have as yet been unable to convert to the production of goods for the private sector. At the same time the industries that are supplying the private sector are, by and large, doing well. Prices are still rising because of an "echo" effect reflecting the big economic noise made by the war and the space program. When the echo dies there will be no big new noise, and when the military oriented output is converted for use in the private sector, there will be adequate capacity. The mutually exclusive conditions of recession and inflation will disappear.

The 1970–1971 recession was similar to the primary postwar recessions of the past (e.g., the recession of 1920–1921). Such recessions have always occurred at the end of the peak war when the economy began to feel the loss of wartime stimulation and the surplus of labor and industrial capacity generated by that loss. The current recession is a confusing one, however, because unlike the peaks of the past, marked by World War I, the Civil War, and to some degree the War of 1812, there has been no sudden peace to shock the economy. There has instead been a slowing down, which has created an economy that has acted less like a desperately sick man than a man with a persistent low-grade infection.

The interdependency of war, inflation, taxes, and federal spending is so complex and so tightly woven that it is easy to see why many observers today doubt that they can all be brought into balance. With the long-wave theory as a base, however, these elements and their economic symptoms may be seen as a syndrome having predictable results. Taxes and their influence on the economy are a key element of that syndrome.

Like inflation, the effects of taxes are generally misunderstood. Consider the amount of money that taxes can raise. If you increase taxes too much you run the risk, in the lower and middle brackets, of a taxpayers' revolt and, in the upper brackets, of sophisticated avoidance. At a long-wave peak, such as the present, the tax burden is usually pushed to the maximum. There is no way, now that the public is turning against wars and space projects, that the present tax structure can survive. But contrary to popular thinking, this change in the rate of taxation will be beneficial. Most discussions about taxes lose sight of the fact that taxes can not be raised beyond a certain point without unproductive results (i.e., unsatisfactory yields in relation to the political and economic risk involved); they also lose sight of the fact that lowering taxes under circumstances of surplus economic capacity (such as a recession) will stimulate the economy as well as actually increase the dollar total of tax revenue. There will be tax reductions in the 1970s to stimulate the economy and, assuming the right kind of tax cuts are made, dollar revenues will rise.

Why? Partly because it happened before under exactly similar circumstances. In the 1920s the federal government cut taxes three times and those cuts, in the years of prosperity and very mild deflation after World War I, stimulated the economy during its recessed periods. It might be simpler, however, just to say that the reason tax cuts benefit the economy is that a man can run faster if you get off his back. Moreover, the right kind of tax cuts could have immeasurable benefits. What the American tax system needs above all is basic reform. It must eliminate the gimmicks, the selective industry-subsidizing deductions, and the application of a progressive tax rate to low-income wage earners, who were never viewed as justifiably includable by the original framers of the progressive income tax.

It is this inclusion of the ordinary wage earner on the progressive-tax ladder that has, surprising though it might seem, contributed to the inflationary pressure of recent years. Economic theory holds that taxes are deflationary because they take money out of the hands of a worker who might spend it. When you examine it, however, that theory is little more than political justification for high taxation. It is valid only if the money is used to pay off existing government debt, not to purchase goods or services in the marketplace. But this is not what happens. When inflation is of greatest concern, during the period of rising prices and interest rates prior to the long-wave peak, increased taxes have not deflated the economy. This is because the government seldom runs a significant surplus during the long-wave upswing, and it is the surplus that provides the funds to retire outstanding debt and cause deflationary pressure on the economy.

If, however, tax money were used just to balance the budget, then the influence of the taxation would be neutral or, technically and for reasons we will not go into, very mildly deflationary. If the tax dollars are spent but the government borrows less as a result, the economy would be stimulated and prices would advance, but not rapidly. But if taxes are increased either by Congress or, more subtly, by an inflation that forces every taxpayer into a high bracket, the added revenues may tempt the government to listen to ever-present warnings about the danger of foreign enemies. When such advice is heeded, armies are built and an ever-rising spiral of rising prices and rising taxes is created.

Taxation under such conditions is highly inflationary

because the government spends the money and borrows more, competing for goods and services in an already straining economy and forcing prices and taxes up further. Increased wages, in turn, force workers into higher tax brackets, far beyond the brackets set up for low-income wage earners before inflation eroded the value of the dollar. Soon wage settlements begin to reflect the *rising cost of taxes,* just as they begin to reflect the rising cost of everything else. Under these conditions, in a strong economy, each rising cost, including the cost of taxes, is bucked along to the consumer. The end result is rapid inflation.

There is a corollary to the inflationary effect of progressive taxation: if the government were forced to vote increased tax revenues, rather than letting the inflation/military-spending/increased-inflation syndrome produce them, it would be virtually impossible to finance wars. If each congressman had to put his hand into his constituents' pockets before the military and its supporters could convince a President and Congress to blunder into foreign adventures, America would fight fewer wars. But inflation and the progressive income tax allow money to be raised without public approval and provide little check on the government.

Another myth closely tied to the long wave is the effect of international trade on the American economy. Most Americans consider competition from abroad a major threat to American industry and to their jobs. Most Americans of course are wrong, but their attitude and their cries for higher tariff barriers are predictable at the peak of the wave. As we showed earlier, the national inclination during years of rising prices and interest rates is toward freer trade and lower tariffs. At the peak, with the first sign of a slow-up, pressure to increase tariffs begins. For a nation so habitually preoccupied with the threat of inflation this is, needless to say, an absurd position. If prices are rising in America because there is too much demand, too many dollars for the goods we produce, why keep out foreign supplies of those goods? Because imports create unemployment? They do not. At worst they cause shifts to those industries with a growing demand for labor.

It is almost as though it were "written" that as the economy goes through the wild boom at the peak and American goods become overpriced, that as a recession develops after the peak-war expansion is terminated, the cry for protection goes up. There was perhaps some excuse for those tariff barriers enacted into law after past peaks, but now the lawmakers should know better. Not only a solid front of economists but years of experience foretell what the outcome will be. But the public and their elected officials ignore this and support tariffs designed to protect American industries that have become fat and/or feeble, even though the farmer, the civil servant, and the white-collar worker will be faced with higher prices. Labor goes along in the belief that tariffs preserve jobs, but a vigorous American economy willing to compete with any nation would do far more for the workingman. The great American ideal of capitalistic competition, of the weak, inefficient participants being weeded out in true laissez-faire style, is lost in the scramble for protection. "Cheap foreign labor" is again being exhumed as the villain, after having rested in peace for two decades, and thus protection returns once more.

CHAPTER 10
THINGS TO COME

Tariffs are here to stay because America is feeling the first pinch of the long-wave downturn. The first part of that downturn, the decade of the seventies, will be prosperous; however, the older, low-technology industries—shoes, textiles, steel—will continue to press for tariff protection. These older industries are given relief from the problems of competing against more modern equipment or lower foreign wages by the long-wave upswing, when good demand and rising prices make it possible to show acceptable profits. The peaking of the long wave, however, takes away this support, and the industries seek relief by trying to exclude foreign competition.

As the downswing in prices and interest rates begins to intensify in the 1980s, an increasing number of industries will begin to feel the pressure that only a few will have felt in the mildly deflationary years of the 1970s. The urge to do the wrong thing will prove irresistible as more industries see their profits narrow because prices fall faster than costs, which are fixed by commitments to plant capacity and to money borrowed long-term to buy that capacity. The temptation to blame foreign imports for one's problems will be too great, as long as a single dollar of sales is lost to the Japanese, the Germans, or the British. Considering the magnitude of the moves made by the Nixon administration to suppress foreign competition at a time when the American economy is clearly not suffering ill effects from that competition, it is not hard to imagine what the reaction would be if unemployment were two or three times its present level.

The war in Vietnam is winding up. Indeed, one is hard pressed to find significant numbers of Americans who argue for anything but withdrawal. Even the hawk-dove disagreements have been reduced to questions of how to withdraw. The very fact that there is no fight left in the hawks will ensure that there will be no more Vietnams for many years. Like the climate following World War I and the Civil War, the ideological climate after Vietnam will be one of rejection of the military. This rejection, combined with public disenchantment with the American space program, already tells us much about the decade of the 1970s.

The military can always be counted on to generate an emergency need to arm—a master plan either to save the country from the threat of foreign domination, to save someone else's country from it, or, under a full head of nationalistic-utopian steam, to impress the homeland's virtues upon some unfortunate nation. These efforts are continuous, just as are the sales promotional efforts of an industrial enterprise. Their success depends on the nation's mood, which for some reason has been warmly receptive at the very beginning and the very end of each long-wave upswing. At other times, particularly during the downswing years, the nation receives the military's demands coldly.

As a result, the years of the coming decades will be peaceful ones, and the military will have to content itself with a garrison life after the great war machine is systematically dismantled. Peace negotiations with the communist block are a necessity because public objection to a unilateral disarmament move would be far too strong. But a combination of peaceful settlements with the Russians and Chinese and a reliance on the overkill potential of each side's thermonuclear arsenal should sustain the situation for some time. It will be the peace of a thermonuclear feudalism, in which the invincible forces will have ceased actively planning to destroy each other.

While today's concern is over the war in Vietnam and how to end it, America's concerns will be far from the military a decade hence. The speed at which major national preoccupations can and usually do shift may be seen in the disappearance of active concern about "the bomb" and the decline in measures to protect mankind against it. In the late fifties and early sixties, thousands of Americans across the nation built private fallout shelters. The collective preparation for war was triggered largely by various international crises—Berlin, Lebanon, Cuba—and the fear that nuclear warfare could start any day. Today, that fear is largely forgotten. As one shelter owner recently commented, according to *The New York Times*, "We're too involved in the immediate needs of today, and those just don't involve the bomb."

The building of bomb shelters was in a real sense the nation preparing for a fight. Kondratieff's theory that wars are fought as rising prosperity brings rising tensions seems to have been proved in the two decades just past. But now, just as private bomb shelters have been abandoned, so too will many of those tensions ease. The daughter of one owner, according to *The New York Times*, splashed red, green, and yellow paint on the drab gray walls and used it for a Halloween party. The will to fight has left and the country's hackles, which recently stood on end in anticipation of doing battle, have been smoothed. The abandonment of private bomb shelters is more than just a reflection of faded concern over the danger of superpowerful weapons, it is the nuclear-age equivalent of beating one's swords into plowshares. The wars are over.

Other problems will similarly fade from public attention. The frantic concern that pollution is actually endangering life on this planet is, for example, misplaced. Of course pollution would endanger mankind's survival if left unchecked, but there is no possibility that it will remain unchecked. We would not be so cocksure if we were not at a long-wave peak, if the present position of the economy were not so ideally situated to attack and solve the pollution problem. All that needs to be done is to redirect the efforts of science and technology into this new field.

Moreover, once everyone is forced to stop polluting, there will be no economic problem, for everyone's costs will be the same. The government will have to step in because only it can provide the legal climate or, in the case of such public polluters as cities and small towns, provide the funds to reduce pollution. The money and the laws will be forthcoming in the 1970s because our efforts will be focused on the environmental issue and because we will have the resources, freed from war expenses, to tackle pollution.

The "youth" problem will also ease during the 1970s. Nowhere are America's fears over the future more misplaced. These worries will dissipate in the seventies because the young will become progressively less vocal in their radicalism, and their elders, while they may not become radicalized, will pick up many of the values they espouse.

The stance of the adult world will relax, too, partly because adults no longer will be subject to attack by their offspring and partly because the new ideas will have been absorbed. Moreover many adults will adopt a young life-style, sufficiently modified to suit the needs of an irrevocably mature world. There will be a strong trend toward a more elegant life and dress, not the black-tie night life of the 1920s but not the turtleneck of the 1960s either. Clothes, furniture, cars, food, and wine will reflect a continuance of high prosperity and gradually declining taxes but the emphasis, while still on youth, will also be on sophistication and taste rather than the frenetic dash to copy the young which we have just experienced. The preoccupation will be on living the good life, which although it implies material things, will rely less on the things themselves to produce happiness.

The music of the seventies will remain substantially unchanged from that of the sixties, at least in the sense that it has reflected the prosperity of the long-wave upswing, its tensions and excitement. In the years of rising excitement that an upswing economy produced, rock music was born and grew, slowly at first, then with gathering momentum, until suddenly it had captured the entire "pop" idiom. Rock symbolized the mood of the late 1950s and the 1960s, and it will continue to symbolize the mood of the 1970s, just as jazz symbolized the period of rising prosperity prior to World War I and the continuation of that prosperity into the 1920s. Action music is a product of prosperity because it serves to relieve the tensions generated in such exciting times. Action dances that accompany the music, such as the Charleston and the black bottom in the last long-wave prosperity and the twist and frug in this upswing, serve as a vehicle of tension release for each individual. The formality of a partner remains as a holdover from music and dances popular in less tension-ridden periods.

The music and the dances of the late 1970s, however, may be slightly calmer than that of the period just past, but only to the degree that the economy is feeling more relaxed after the trauma of the long-wave peak that we are now enduring. At the beginning of the seventies, in the midst of the primary postwar recession, the music became moody and introspective, reflecting a public mood far different from the upbeat, expansive, rebellious mood of a few years before. The latter part of the seventies will clearly change this, and the tone will reflect the new national preoccupation—to have fun. Early rock was a joyful and unique release from the traditions of the downswing years, which were still hanging on and were totally inappropriate for the "turned-on" posture the upswing years assumed. As the peak years unfolded, war, riot, inflation, and protest clouded the new-found exuberance that prosperity had brought just a few years before, and the main thrust of popular music reflected the currents of protest flowing throughout society. When the peak and its accompanying ills have been passed, music and dance will once again reflect the urge to have fun, to be more concerned with personal pleasures than national issues.

If music of the 1970s will reflect the post-peak mood, so will clothes. There is no doubt that what has been referred to as "the costume party" will come to an end. Nevertheless the clothes of the 1970s will make a marked progression, along with the economy and the mind of the public, toward being less intense and more sophisticated. The fall 1971 issue of *Gentlemen's Quarterly*, for example, features a front-page announcement that "the costume party is over." Accompanying that line is the picture of a gentleman whose appearance presumably backs up that statement. He is wearing a broad-brimmed hat, patterned shirt and tie and a wide lapel jacket. His overall color scheme is a long, long way from Brooks Brothers conservatism. If one had viewed his clothes a decade ago, the natural reaction probably would have been that the costume party had just begun!

In the 1960s clothing followed the mood of the young —excited, rebellious, different from the past. Above all it served as a uniform of identification with the new movement; clothes were a badge that said "we are no longer trying to look like our elders, we are rebelling, we are in charge of our own destiny." As adults, caught in the excited tempo of rising prosperity, began adopting the styles of the young, it became necessary for clothes to be even more "far out" in order to remain at arm's length from the adult world.

For many, the adoption of youthful clothing styles was only an outward manifestation of the adoption of a whole life-style. While there were probably aspects that individual adults could not swallow, there was on the whole an effort to emulate youth. It may have varied from person to person, but the differences were chiefly a matter of degree.

The decade of the 1970s will resemble the decade of the 1960s in that it will be one of relatively high prosperity. But the seventies will be distinct in that the unpleasant aspects of the long-wave upswing will be absent. The seventies will be very much like the 1920s but, to understand that comparison while viewing the future, it is necessary for one to look at the twenties from the 1919 side rather than from the 1930 side. We have come to think of the twenties as meaning bathtub gin, jazz, speakeasies, and a wild stock market. From the 1919 end it looked more like a relief from such things as war, inflation, strikes, riots, and bombings. The 1920s were also a time when the nation recovered from a severe post–World War I recession, the military establishment was systematically dismantled, trade protection was instituted, politics were forgotten, and the country turned its back on the rest of the world.

The nation was tired at the beginning of the 1920s, just as it is now, and for the same reasons. But when the problems of the peak years were solved or otherwise removed, Americans were able to enjoy life in a truly unique period—the plateau-like decade between two decades of upswing and two of downswing. It felt very good, so good, in fact, that in the later years of the decade a feeling of euphoria set in. The new era, it was thought, had arrived. The economy would never turn down. Life would always be good. What really happened is the history that everyone knows.

In the ten years to come, America will be a very different place than it has been for a long time; it will be in the middle of that one decade in five when there is high prosperity, full employment, no inflation, and peace and plenty. These good things will happen under exactly the same conditions under which they have occurred before, but it will all seem different.

The public attitude toward marijuana during the 1970s will not be unlike that toward alcohol in the 1920s. At the beginning of the "Noble Experiment," as Prohibition was called, most Americans felt that banning alcohol was a good thing. But drinking became more fashionable than ever, for Prohibition added the flavor of the forbidden. Moreover, as Americans of all ages turned from Victorianism after World War I, they groped for new values. Drinking, along with bobbed hair, short skirts, and jazz, was eagerly flaunted as a symbol of liberation. Marijuana is assuming the same role fifty years later. In the 1960s, its use was largely confined to the young. In the 1970s, its use will spread to all age groups.

No one can discuss the 1920s without the 1930s eventually creeping in, and no one can draw an analogy between the 1920s and the 1970s without the question of an analogy between the 1930s and the 1980s being raised. Such discussions are never popular. People tend to present reasons why history cannot repeat itself, and there is almost a tone of willing it not to happen in their voices. Perhaps it will not. Maybe in the 1970s the United States will see continued inflation, unbalanced budgets, more foreign military adventures, continued domestic unrest, with senseless bombings, confrontation politics, and riots in the streets, but we doubt it. If such things do happen, however, then fear not, because it will mean that the Kondratieff wave is only a statistical illusion, and that the chances of a serious depression in the 1980s are slim. But if the predictions for the middle and late 1970s come true, as the predictions for the late 1960s did, then the conclusion is inescapable—sometime in the early 1980s the effects of the long-wave downswing should begin to be felt.

There are two opposing though not mutually exclusive feelings about the secondary postwar recession, or depression, if you use the traditional term. The first is that such depressions, which begin about a decade after the peak war's end, have been of increasing intensity. Always protracted, the three such downturns on record —1824 after the War of 1812, 1874 after the Civil War, and 1929 after World War I—grew in severity, though not in duration. The most logical explanation of this accelerating intensity is the growing complexity of the industrial society, our march toward a money economy. With more people dependent on wages, jobs, spending, and corporate organization, a downturn would tend to hit harder. There were, for example, fewer chickens in the backyards of households in the 1930s than there had been in the 1870s. In the 1980s there will perhaps be none at all.

The other possibility is that the government can minimize the effects of depression through sound economic management and use of such stabilizers as unemployment compensation, public works projects, and deficit spending.

Actually, what will probably happen is a combination of both possibilities. The increasing complexity of our society, with its production-consumption orientation, must make it increasingly vulnerable in a downturn. At the same time, the built-in stabilizers would soften the blow, and compensatory measures would assist in bringing us out. But we cannot assume from this that we are not going to get into a depression. It has become fashionable to say that we cannot prevent minor recessions, but that we have solved the question of major downturns. This idea survives only because the recessions of the upswing decades are always relatively mild. The current recession, which equates to the primary post-peak-war recessions of the past, has been the longest and toughest to cure since downturns of the 1930s and we are not even out of the war yet! Had the wartime stimulation been withdrawn completely and suddenly, as it was after World War I and the other peak wars, it would have blown the "no more serious downturns" notion to bits.

The other important point to consider about a major downturn is the difference between preventing it and curing it. We do not doubt that a depression can be cured, although it was difficult to do in the 1930s. Next time, mobilizing the compensatory forces will be an easier matter—we already know what should be done. But the problem, as before, will be actually determining that we are having a depression. It took three years after the 1929 stock-market crash for the people of the United States to realize how serious conditions were, and that was only when the depression had finally hit bottom. The euphoria of the late 1920s so conditioned people to believe in the new era of unending prosperity that they could not accept the fact that it had ended. What complicated things then, and probably will do so again, is that the very worst of times were preceded by the very best of times.

The possibility that the automatic stabilizers will prevent a major downturn is, as we have implied, remote at best. The problem is compounded because the economy will be perfectly set up for such a depression by the early 1980s just as it was at the end of the 1920s. A few years of balanced budgets, the end of the upward reinforcing spiral, plenty of industrial capacity (which was built with money borrowed at relatively high interest rates), and a couple of tax cuts should set the stage. Without the push from the upswing of prices, a war, or large federal deficits, the long-wave downswing will take over. There is little possibility of avoiding the consequences of the downturn in prices and interest rates that should begin in earnest in the 1980s. There is simply no possibility of convincing enough of the public of a coming downturn to make preventive measures politically feasible. Indeed, in the euphoria and contentment of the late 1970s and early 1980s, a downturn will seem ridiculous. The past two decades are littered with the bones of economists and others who have predicted disaster, who have harkened back to 1929 and shown the similarities with "today." The decade to come will be no exception, until the end, when the voices will at last be still. "Depression— preposterous!"

The point of this book is not to frighten the reader with a look at what we believe will happen in the 1980s any more than it is to delight you with our ideas that the decade to come will provide relief from the most pressing problems of today. Nor is it written from the colossally arrogant belief that we—the authors—might somehow prevent what looks to us to be an impending economic disaster. Rather, our object is to bring the role of the long wave to the forefront, to speculate about what will happen based on what has happened in the past, and to begin to look at the underlying cause, a thread that runs through it all. If there will be a depression in the 1980s, which we think there will, we should plan to use it constructively by spending large sums to solve the problems of housing, transportation, and education and to restore the damage done to the earth. We must not let a depression shake our logic or make us lose faith in the basic viability of our economic system. In the last great downturn America was lucky because we did not attempt to destroy our system out of despair, and, though we as a people drew some highly inaccurate conclusions as to the causes of the Great Depression, we did not burn our ship because it had temporarily run aground.

It is our hope that this book will stimulate inquiry into the true causes of the economic downturn of the 1980s and perhaps provide an understanding of the broad and hidden economic forces that govern our economy. We feel that such an understanding is especially important now, when faith in our existing institutions has been cast into doubt.

BIBLIOGRAPHY

ALLEN, FREDERICK LEWIS. *Only Yesterday: An Informal History of the Nineteen Twenties.* New York: Harper and Brothers, 1931.

———. *The Big Change: America Transforms Itself, 1900–1950.* New York: Harper & Row, First Perennial Library Edition, 1969.

COWLEY, MALCOLM. *Exiles Return.* New York: Viking Press, 1951.

FIRESTON, JOHN M. *Federal Receipts and Expenditures During Business Cycles, 1879–1958.* Princeton, N.J.: Princeton University Press, 1960.

GRAS, N. S. B., and LARSEN, HENRIETTA. *Case Book in American Business History.* New York: F. S. Crofts & Company, 1939.

KIMMEL, LEWIS. *Federal Budget and Fiscal Policy, 1789–1958.* Washington, D.C.: Brookings Institute, 1959.

MACAULLAY, FREDERICK R. *Some Theoretical Problems Suggested by the Movements of Interest Rates, Bond Yields and Stock Prices in the United States Since 1856.* New York: National Bureau of Economic Research, 1938.

PERLMAN, SELIG. *A History of Trade Unionism in the United States.* New York: Macmillan Co., 1923.

POTTER, DAVID M. *People of Plenty.* Chicago: University of Chicago Press, 1954.

REICH, CHARLES A. *The Greening of America.* New York: Random House, 1970.

SAMUELSON, PAUL A. *Economics: An Introductory Analysis.* 5th ed. New York: McGraw-Hill, 1961.

SCHUMPETER, JOSEPH A. *Business Cycles.* vol. 1. New York: McGraw-Hill, 1939.

SMITH, WALTER B., and COLE, ARTHUR H. *Fluctuations in American Business, 1790–1860.* Cambridge, Massachusetts: Harvard University Press, 1935.

STUDENSKI, PAUL, KROOSS, HERMAN E. *Financial History of the United States.* New York: McGraw-Hill, 1952.

SULLIVAN, MARK. *Our Times: The United States, 1900–1925.* 6 vols. New York: Scribner, 1926–1935.

WARREN, G. F., and PEARSON, F. A. *Wholesales Prices for 213 Years, 1720 to 1932.* Ithaca, New York: Cornell University Press, 1932.

WICKER, ELMUS R. *Federal Reserve Monetary Policy, 1917–1933.* New York: Random House, 1966.

WYLLIE, I. G. *The Self Made Man in America: The Myth of Rags to Riches.* New Brunswick, N.J.: Rutgers University Press, 1954.